WriteTraits®
TEACHER'S GUIDE

Vicki Spandel

Grade 2

GReaT S✦uRCe®
EDUCATION GROUP
A Houghton Mifflin Company

Vicki Spandel

Vicki Spandel was codirector of the original teacher team that developed the six-trait model and has designed instructional materials for all grade levels. She has written several books, including *Creating Writers—Linking Writing Assessment and Instruction* (Longman), and is a former language arts teacher, journalist, technical writer, consultant, and scoring director for dozens of state, county, and district writing assessments.

Cover: Illustration by Claude Martinot Design.

Design: The Mazer Corporation

Printed in the United States of America

International Standard Book Number: 0-669-50477-7

3 4 5 6 7 8 9 10 - MZ - 08 07 06 05

Contents

Introduction

Unit 1: Ideas

Unit 2: Organization

Unit 3: Voice

Unit 4: Word Choice

Unit 5: Sentence Fluency

Unit 6: Conventions

Welcome to the World of Traits!

With the *Write Traits® Classroom Kit*, we offer you a way to teach writing that helps students understand what good writing is and how to achieve it. The kit provides instruction in six traits of effective writing. The term *trait*, as it is used here, refers to a characteristic or quality that defines writing. The six traits include: ideas, organization, voice, word choice, sentence fluency, conventions.

We recognize that many primary students do not revise or edit their writing. Don't worry! The six-trait model offers a step-by-step approach that eases beginning writers into all steps of the writing process and builds an inside-out understanding of how that process works. The lessons within this kit are based on the following beliefs:

√ Even the youngest students can write.

√ Even the youngest writers can revise—if we accept small changes as significant.

√ Even the youngest writers can edit—if we give them editorial tasks appropriate to their ability.

√ Even beginning readers can be thoughtful evaluators when they listen, using their ears as well as their eyes to respond to text.

√ One of the most important things we can teach our young writers is writers' language because it empowers them to think and work as writers.

Six-trait instruction is designed to support the writing process by giving students a language for thinking about writing and by breaking writing, revising, and editing into small, manageable tasks. Even if you have never worked with the six traits, you are likely to find them familiar because they are the foundation of good writing.

Components in the Write Traits® Classroom Kit

Each *Write Traits® Classroom Kit* contains the following components:

Teacher's Guide

The Teacher's Guide takes you step-by-step through each part of the program, from introducing traits to presenting lessons to wrap-up activities that bring all the traits together. The Teacher's Guide also contains reproducible rubrics and sample papers for practicing scoring and revising.

Student Traitbook

The Student Traitbook contains all the practice exercises for the six traits. It is available as a copymaster within the kit or can be purchased for every student. We recommend the purchase of individual Traitbooks for any teacher wishing to create student portfolios.

Posters

Hang the posters for students as a handy reference when writing, revising, or editing.

Self-stick Note Pads (package of 5)

Use these handy self-stick notes so that you won't have to write directly on students' papers.

Overhead Transparencies

Use the transparencies for whole-class response to and discussion of the Sample Papers in the back of the Teacher's Guide.

Writing Pocket

Available for purchase for every student, this writing folder provides a place for students to store their writing.

Teaching the Traits Units

The Teacher's Guide is organized into six units, one for each of the six traits. Each unit includes an overview, four lessons specifically designed to build strengths in that trait, and a unit wrap-up. At the end of the book are sample papers that illustrate strengths and problems related to each trait. Your students can "score" the sample papers (matching each one to the **Made it!**, **Getting there...**, or **It's a start.** level). You can also use them as a basis for classroom discussions on what makes writing work.

Unit Overviews

Each of the six unit overviews accomplishes the following:

- defines the trait
- describes the instruction
- summarizes each lesson
- contains two rubrics (one for the teacher, one for the student)
- recommends literature that can be used to model the trait

Traits Lessons

All twenty-four lessons, four for each of the six traits, follow the same format:

- Introduction, which includes an objective, skills focus, and suggested time frame
- Setting Up the Lesson, which highlights main concepts and suggests strategies for engaging students
- Teaching the Lesson, which provides strategies and answers to material in the Student Traitbook

- Extending the Lesson, which offers optional activities at two levels (beginning writer and advanced writer) to expand students' skills and enrich their understanding of the lesson

Each lesson incorporates at least two (and sometimes all) of the following elements:

√ Listening

√ Drawing

√ Talking

√ Writing

Unit Summaries

Each of the six unit summaries does the following:

- reviews characteristics of the trait
- provides students an opportunity to read and understand the rubric
- invites students to use the rubric in responding to sample papers

Warm-up Activities

Warm-up activities encourage students to think like writers right from the start. These activities are designed to help students read and listen like writers, noticing the specific qualities (traits) that make writing work and the kinds of changes writers make when they revise.

Wrap-up Activities

The wrap-up activities provide closure by bringing all six traits together in short review lessons. These activities are designed to help you see whether your students understand the traits and are ready to use them in their own writing, revising, and editing.

Using the Rubrics

At this level, rubrics are not number-based. Rather, they contain descriptors to define performance at each of three levels:

Made it!
A level of proficiency at which the student writer is communicating with the reader

Getting there . . .
About halfway home, a level at which writing shows many strengths but still needs some work

It's a start.
A beginning level—the student has put something on paper, however rudimentary

The main objectives at this primary level of trait-based instruction are to

- increase students' understanding of and use of writers' language

- extend the amount of writing students feel comfortable doing

- help students develop an "ear" for what works well in writing

- build students' confidence in themselves as writers

While these rubrics are *not* designed for use in large-scale assessment, you will find their checklist approach well suited to classroom assessment and to the use of portfolios that show students' growth as writers over time.

Students have their own version of the rubrics, written in student-friendly, simple language that you and they can read together until they feel ready to read the rubrics on their own. At that point, the rubrics serve as a guide to good writing and revision.

Differences Among Rubrics

Rubrics define performance along a continuum from beginning through developing and proficient levels. Some rubrics have numbers to signify levels of performance: 1 through 4, or 1 through 5 or 6. Other rubrics use descriptors, as is the case with our primary level rubrics. We have chosen descriptors because we believe they are more meaningful to students than numbers.

If you wish to use numbers (for grading purposes), the rubrics can easily be adapted to either 5-point or 6-point scales. The "Made it!" level can be defined as a 5 or a 5–6 split, depending on the scale. The "Getting there..." level is a 3 on a 5-point scale, or a 3–4 split on a 6-point scale. The "It's a start." level is a 1 on a 5-point scale, or a 1–2 split on a 6-point scale. You do not need to worry about numbers unless you are using the scales for grading purposes and need a point total to compute grades. Check the appendix in the Teacher's Guide for adapted rubrics with numbers.

Sample Papers

The Sample Papers have been carefully selected to match the grade level at which your students are writing. Some papers are informational while others are narrative. Some are well done; others reflect moderate to serious problems. These "in process" papers offer an excellent opportunity for students to practice revision skills. Ask your students to revise as many papers as time permits. This extended practice provides an excellent lead-in to revision of their own work. Your primary students can "practice revision" by actually writing or by simply offering suggestions about how a paper could be improved.

Suggested responses based on the 3-level rubric are provided for each paper. These scores are *suggestions*—and cannot be more. They reflect the thoughtful reading and responses of trained teachers, but they should not be considered the only correct "answers."

Frequently Asked Questions

How did this six-trait approach get started?

The *Write Traits® Classroom Kit* is based on the original six-trait model of writing instruction and assessment developed in 1984 by teachers in the Beaverton, Oregon, School District. Because it has been widely embraced by teachers at all grade levels, kindergarten through college, the model has spread throughout the country—and much of the world. Traits themselves, of course, have been around as long as writing itself since writers have always needed sound, intriguing ideas, good organization, powerful voice, and so on. What is *new* is using consistent language with students to define writing at various levels of performance.

As a teacher, how can I make this program work for my students?

You can do several important things:

- Provide significant time for writing. Process-based writing is foundational to writing instruction, and the six traits are most effective in classrooms where students write often and for different purposes and where they share their writing.

- Look to your students for answers; let them tell *you* what makes a piece of writing work (or not work), prior to sharing your own thoughts.

- Share many different kinds of writing with students, including the student samples from this kit; professional writing from books, newspapers, advertisements, and other sources; and your own writing.

- Be a writer yourself, modeling steps within the writing process, and encouraging students to use their increasing knowledge of traits to coach you.

- Give students their own writing rubrics as you introduce each trait. Students should use the rubrics to respond to others' writing and as a guide to their own writing and revision.

- Share copies of rubrics with parents. This encourages them to use writers' language with their children. It also helps them know what you are looking for as you assess and respond to their children's work.

Can 6-trait instruction/assessment take the place of the writing process?

Absolutely not! The 6-trait approach is meant to enhance and enrich a process-based approach to writing. Along with a wide set of options for revising, it gives students a language for talking and thinking like writers. Often students (of all ages—not only primary) do not revise their writing thoroughly (or at all) because they don't know what to do. Students who know the six traits have no difficulty thinking of ways to revise their writing. **Note:** At the primary level, revision may be as simple as adding one detail or changing the word order in one sentence. Any thoughtful change qualifies as a form of revision and is a vital steppingstone to more in-depth and expansive changes the student will attempt at later grade levels.

What do I do if I don't know a lot about the writing process?

Don't worry. We can help. First, you may wish to read the brief article by Jeff Hicks that summarizes the writing process. It appears on page xv of this Teacher's Guide. This article will give you all the basic information and terminology you need. If you would like to know more, refer to the Teacher Resources, page xviii. These resources will give you a strong background in the basics of the writing process, even if you've never been to a single workshop on the subject!

What do I have to give up from my current curriculum?

Nothing. If you are teaching writing through writers' workshops or any writing process-based approach, you will find that virtually everything you do is compatible with six-trait writing. Trait-based instruction does not replace process writing but supports it. Moreover, you can mix our lessons with your favorite writing activities and literature, and the result will be a powerful writing curriculum. **Remember:** If you are teaching writing, you are teaching traits—as you work on details, organization, leads and endings, good word choice, strong sentences. The traits simply give you a language for clarifying what you are already teaching!

Do I have to teach the traits in order?

We recommend that you teach both traits and lessons in the order presented because we use a sequential approach in which skills build on one another. Longer writing activities toward the end of each unit require students to use the skills they have learned in a previous unit so that nothing is "lost." In other words, we do not want students to forget about *ideas* just because they move on to *organization*.

We recognize that most teachers prefer to teach conventions throughout the course of instruction, rather than as a separate unit. Therefore, feel free to incorporate instruction in conventions as you present the other traits.

Do all six traits ever come together?

Definitely. Writing should not be disjointed. Taking it apart into traits makes it manageable. Eventually though, all these skills come together for a smooth ride. With this in mind, the Wrap-Up Activities serve to review and reinforce all six traits. You can use this opportunity to check your students' progress towards working with all of them.

Using Traits with the Writing Process

by Jeff Hicks

If writing were an act of fairytale magic or a matter of wishing, the word *process* would never apply to what people do when they write. All writers would have to do is wave their magic wands, rub their enchanted lamps to make their genies appear, or catch the one fish, from an ocean filled with fish, that grants wishes to the lucky person who hauls it in. *I'd like a bestseller about a pig and a spider who live on a farm. Allakazam! Presto! Newbery Medal!* Perhaps Roald Dahl was a fisherman and Beverly Cleary was a collector of antique lamps, right? Of course not! Writers understand that writing is a process involving multiple steps and plenty of time. An understanding of the process of writing is an important foundation for all young writers. Once they have the process in place, students can grasp and use the six traits of writing to help them revise and assess their own work. The six traits support the writing process.

The Writing Process The traditional view of the writing process is one that involves four or five steps or stages.

> **Prewriting**
> **Drafting (Writing)**
> **Revising**
> **Editing**
> **Publishing/Sharing**

1. **Prewriting**—This is the stage in which the writer attempts to find a topic, narrow it, and map out a plan. The writer usually isn't concerned with creating whole sentences or paragraphs at this point. Prewriting is done *before* the writer begins to write, and it is aimed at defining an idea and getting it rolling.

2. **Drafting** (Writing)—In this stage, the writer's idea begins to come to life. Sentences and paragraphs begin to take shape. The writer may experiment with different leads. In this stage, writers need to know that they can change directions, cross out words or sentences, and draw arrows to link details that are out of sequence. The term *rough draft*, or *first draft,* refers to writers in motion, changing directions and letting their ideas take shape.

3. **Revising**—When writers revise, their topics and ideas come into focus. In this stage, writers do a great deal of math—adding or subtracting single words, phrases, or entire paragraphs. What to revise often becomes clearer to students if they have had some time away from their drafts. Putting a draft away, out of sight and mind, for a few days or even more, may provide a sharper focus on weak areas. A writer might even ask, "Did I really write this?" The efforts made at revision will easily separate strong writing from weak writing.

4. **Editing**—This stage is all about making a piece of writing more accessible to readers. In this stage, writers fine-tune their work by focusing on correct punctuation, capitalization, grammar, usage, and paragraphing. Writers will want to be open to all the technological help (spell checker, for example) and human help they can find.

5. **Publishing/Sharing**—Not every piece of writing reaches this stage. The term *sharing* refers here to something more public than the kind of interactive sharing that should be happening at the previous stages. When writing is going to be "published" in the classroom or put on display as finished work, it needs to have been carefully selected as a piece of writing that has truly experienced all the other stages of the writing process.

These steps are often presented in classrooms as being separate, mutually exclusive events. *If I'm prewriting, I can't be revising. If I'm drafting, I can't be editing. If I'm revising, I can't be editing.* Mature writers know that the process may proceed through the steps in linear fashion, one at a time, but it is more likely that the parts of the process will intertwine. The process doesn't seem so overwhelming if a young writer can gain this perspective. I like to teach students several prewriting strategies—webbing, outlining, making word caches, drawing, and developing a list of questions—but I also like to show them through my own writing that prewriting and drafting can occur simultaneously. Having students experience their teacher as a writer is the most powerful way to demonstrate the importance of each stage and how it connects with the others. For instance, the best way for me to prewrite is to begin "writing." It is the act of writing (drafting) that often gets my ideas flowing better than if I tried to make a web of the idea. Writing also allows me to demonstrate that I can revise at any time. I can cross out a sentence, change a word, draw an arrow to place a sentence in a different paragraph, add a few words, or move a whole paragraph; all of this can be done while I draft an idea. At the same time, I might even notice that I need to fix the spelling of a word or add a period—that's editing!

Bringing in the Traits I know that many young writers speak and act as if they have magical pens or pencils. In the classroom, these are the students who proclaim, "I'm done!" minutes after beginning, or they are the ones who say, "But I like it the way it is!" when faced with a teacher's suggestion to tell a bit more or to make a few changes. Other students frequently complain, "I don't have anything to write about." Immersing these students in the writing process with a teacher who is also a writer is the clearest path to silencing these comments. Throw into this mix a strong understanding of the six traits of writing, and you are well on your way to creating passionate, self-assessing writers.

Teacher Resources

The "Must-Have" List for Teaching Writing Using the Six Traits

Avery, Carol. 2002. *And With a Light Touch*. 2nd edition. Portsmouth, NH: Heinemann.

Burdett, Lois. 2002. *Shakespeare Can Be Fun* (series). Willowdale, Ontario, and Buffalo, NY: Firefly Books.

Calkins, Lucy McCormick. 1994. *The Art of Teaching Writing*. 2nd edition. Portsmouth, NH: Heinemann.

Cramer, Ronald L. 2001. *Creative Power: The Nature and Nurture of Children's Writing*. New York: Addison Wesley Longman.

Fletcher, Ralph. 1993. *What a Writer Needs*. Portsmouth, NH: Heinemann.

Fletcher, Ralph and Joann Portalupi. 1998. *Craft Lessons: Teaching Writing K–8*. Portland, Maine: Stenhouse Publishers.

Fox, Mem. 1993. *Radical Reflections: Passionate Opinions on Teaching, Learning, and Living*. New York: Harcourt, Brace & Company.

Frank, Marjorie. 1995. *If You're Trying to Teach Kids How to Write . . . you've gotta have this book!* 2nd ed. Nashville: Incentive Publications, Inc.

Freeman, Marcia S. 1998. *Teaching the Youngest Writers*. Gainesville, FL: Maupin House.

Glynn, Carol. 2001. *Learning on Their Feet: A Sourcebook for Kinesthetic Learning Across the Curriculum K–8*. Shoreham, VT: Discover Writing Press.

Graves, Donald H. 1986. *Writing: Teachers and Children At Work*. Portsmouth, NH: Heinemann.

Johnson, Bea. 1999. *Never Too Early to Write*. Gainesville, FL: Maupin House.

Keene, Ellen Oliver, with Susan Zimmerman. *Mosaic of Thought: Teaching Comprehension in a Reader's Workshop*. 1997. Portsmouth, NH: Heinemann.

Kemper, Dave, Ruth Nathan, Patrick Sebranek, and Carol Elsholz. 2000. *Write Away*. Wilmington, MA: Great Source Education Group. (Full program includes a *Program Guide, SkillsBook, Student Handbook, and Teacher's Guide.*)

Lane, Barry. 1993. *after THE END*. Portsmouth, NH: Heinemann.

Lane, Barry. 1998. *The Reviser's Toolbox*. Shoreham, VT: Discover Writing Press.

Newkirk, Thomas. 1989. *More Than Stories: The Range of Children's Writing*. Portsmouth, NH: Heinemann.

Portalupi, Joann, with Ralph Fletcher. 2001. *Nonfiction Craft Lessons: Teaching Information Writing K–8*. Portland, ME: Stenhouse Publishers.

Romano, Tom. 1995. *Writing With Passion: Life Stories, Multiple Genres*. Portsmouth, NH: Boynton/Cook Publishers.

Routman, Regie. 2000. *Conversations*. Portsmouth, NH: Heinemann.

Slonim, Nancy Aronie. 1998. *Writing From the Heart*. New York: Hyperion.

Spandel, Vicki. 2001. *Creating Writers*. 3rd ed. New York: Allyn & Bacon.

Spandel, Vicki. 2003. *Creating Young Writers*. New York: Allyn & Bacon.

Spandel, Vicki, with Ruth Nathan and Laura Robb. 2003. *Daybook of Critical Reading and Writing, Grade 2*. Wilmington, MA: Great Source Education Group.

Steele, Bob. 1998. *Draw Me a Story*. Winnipeg, Manitoba: Peguis Publishers.

Stiggins, Richard J. 2000. *Student-Centered Classroom Assessment*. 3rd ed. Upper Saddle River, NJ: Prentice-Hall.

Strickland, Kathleen and James Strickland. 2000. *Making Assessment Elementary*. Portsmouth, NH: Heinemann.

Thomason, Tommy. 1993. *More Than a Writing Teacher: How to Become a Teacher Who Writes*. Commerce, TX: Bridge Press.

Thomason, Tommy. 1998. *Writer to Writer: How to Conference Young Authors*. Norwood, MA: Christopher Gordon Publishers.

Using Write Traits Classroom Kits with Write Away

Write Traits Classroom Kit, Grade 2	Skill Focus	Write Away© 2002
Unit 1: Ideas		
Lesson 1: The Word and Picture Team	Connecting ideas and pictures	Making Picture Dictionaries pp. 111–113
Lesson 2: What's the BIG Idea?	Getting the message	Keeping an Idea Notebook, pp. 29–31
Lesson 3: Wanted: Good Details!	Choosing interesting details	Gathering Ideas, p. 33
Lesson 4: Sticking with It	Focusing on the topic	Planning Your Writing, pp. 32–33
Unit 2: Organization		
Lesson 5: Just Like a Puzzle	Building up details	Writing the First Draft, pp. 34–35
Lesson 6: Starting Off with a Bang!	Writing strong leads	Writing a News Story, pp. 94–95
Lesson 7: One Story at a Time	Staying on topic	Making a Story Map, p. 237
Lesson 8: The Finish Line	Wrapping up	Ending, p. 39
Unit 3: Voice		
Lesson 9: An Ear for Voice	Comparing authors' voices	Personal Voice, p. 26
Lesson 10: A Bouquet of Voices	Finding words to describe authors' voices	Telling Stories, pp. 226–229
Lesson 11: Hear Me Roar!	Expressing your own voice	Writing in Journals, pp. 65–66
Lesson 12: More Voice, Please!	Improving your voice	Writing an All-About-Me Story, pp. 78–79

Unit 4: Word Choice		
Lesson 13: Oh, Not Again!	Avoiding repetition	Well-Chosen Words, p. 26
Lesson 14: Verb Power	Sharpening your verbs	Verbs, p. 281
Lesson 15: Use the Clues	Valuing reading as a source for new words	Reading to Understand, pp. 182–187
Lesson 16: Tickling the Senses	Appreciating sensory words	Describing a Subject, p. 235
Unit 5: Sentence Fluency		
Lesson 17: Keep It Rolling	Creating fluency	Sentence Parts, p. 52
Lesson 18: Making Changes	Varying sentence starters	What Is a Paragraph? p. 57
Lesson 19: Come On, Let's Hear It!	Reading aloud and listening	Performing Stories, pp. 220–221
Lesson 20: Math—A Big PLUS for Writing	Combining choppy sentences	Writing Longer Sentences, pp. 54–55
Unit 6: Conventions		
Lesson 21: Telling or Asking?	Understanding punctuation	Using Punctuation, p. 249
Lesson 22: Tools of the Trade	Using editor's marks	Checking for Errors, pp. 42–43
Lesson 23: Capitals at the Start	Finding missing capitals	Use Capital Letters, pp. 257–258
Lesson 24: I Know It on Sight!	Spotting careless errors	Spelling Tips, pp. 268–269

Write Traits® Classroom Kits SCOPE AND SEQUENCE

Trait/Skill	Grade 2	3	4	5	6	7	8
IDEAS							
Narrowing the Topic				•	•	•	•
Getting Started	•	•	•		•		•
Identifying the Main Idea	•	•	•	•			
Clarifying Ideas					•	•	•
Expanding Sketchy Writing					•	•	
Identifying What Is Important		•	•	•			
Making Writing Concise		•	•			•	•
ORGANIZATION							
Writing a Strong Lead	•	•	•	•			
Putting Things in Order	•	•		•		•	
Identifying Organizational Patterns			•		•		•
Matching Organizational Pattern and Writing Task			•		•		•
Staying on Topic	•	•		•		•	
Creating Strong Transitions					•	•	•
Writing Endings	•	•	•	•			
Putting Details Together					•	•	•
VOICE							
Defining Voice	•				•	•	•
Matching Voice and Purpose		•		•		•	
Putting Voice into Personal Narrative		•	•	•			
Putting Voice into Expository Writing					•	•	•
Matching Voice to Audience					•	•	•
Sharing Favorite Voices		•	•	•			
Putting Voice into Flat Writing	•				•		•
Using Personal Voice	•	•	•	•			

Trait/Skill	Grade						
	2	3	4	5	6	7	8
WORD CHOICE							
Using Strong Verbs	•	•	•	•			
Using Synonyms and Antonyms to Enhance Meaning					•	•	•
Inferring Meaning from Context		•	•	•			
Using Sensory Words to Create a Word Picture	•	•	•	•	•		•
Using Strong Words to Revise Flat Writing					•	•	•
Revising Overwritten Language			•		•	•	•
Eliminating Wordiness		•		•			•
SENTENCE FLUENCY							
Making Choppy Writing Fluent	•	•		•		•	
Varying Sentence Beginnings	•	•	•				•
Varying Sentence Length	•			•	•	•	
Eliminating Run-ons		•	•		•		
Inserting Transitions					•	•	•
Creating Dialogue		•	•	•			
Assessing Fluency Through Interpretive Reading	•		•		•		•
Reading and Revising Personal Text				•		•	•
CONVENTIONS							
Distinguishing Between Revision and Editing			•	•	•	•	•
Spotting Errors	•	•		•		•	
Knowing the Symbols	•	•	•	•	•	•	•
Correcting Errors	•	•	•	•	•	•	•
Creating an Editing Checklist		•	•		•		•

Warm-up Activity 1

What Changed?

For use with *Student Traitbook*, pages v–vi

The purpose of the warm-up activity is to encourage students to notice differences in the two pieces of writing so they can begin to think about what makes good writing work. Students don't need to be familiar with the six traits to do this exercise. The activity will take about 20 minutes.

Explain that writers sometimes change their writing if they remember details or think of a better way to say something. Then, read the **Before** and **After** samples of "Ben and His Cat" aloud as students follow along. When you finish reading, ask students what kinds of changes the writer made to make the **After** sample more fun to read. Students can work with a partner on this warm-up activity.

Ben and His Cat

How do students like this story? Ask for their comments and write them on an overhead. Then, read the revised version (the **After** version) aloud as students follow along. **Note:** The **After** version is longer and more complex. If students have difficulty following along, it is fine for them just to listen as you read. Or you can read it more than once to help them become comfortable with the language.

Comments

The writer makes several kinds of changes. Most apparent is the fact that the **After** version is longer! Longer is not always better! In this case, however, adding more text lets the writer add details about how he felt, why he doesn't like going to the store, playing with Chloe, and the special treats he picks out at the store. In addition, this version is much livelier than the first. The **Before** version simply reports what happened. In the **After** version, the writer seems to have a good time telling the story of Ben and his cat. This is *voice*. We also get some interesting *word choice* that does not appear in the first version: *whizzing around the corners, crashing, stalking him through the jungle of his bedroom,* and *fret.*

What Do You Notice?

NOTE: Activity may be repeated if you choose more than one book.

This Warm-up Activity is designed to give students an opportunity to begin thinking like assessors in responding to literature. For this activity, you will need:

√ One or more picture books (you can choose any titles you like)

√ A blank overhead transparency and overhead pen for making notes

Students will listen as you read a text aloud. As you read, encourage students to think about what they notice or what they like about the book. They should look at the pictures as well as listen to the text. Pictures display a great deal of detail and voice. In addition, the coordination between pictures and text in a picture book is a critical feature of organization. When students say, "The pictures go with the story," they are commenting on this connection.

Tell students that when you finish reading, you will ask for their comments and thoughts.

Ask questions like these to bring out additional comments:

√ Does anyone remember a favorite word from the book? (This question makes a link to WORD CHOICE.)

√ Close your eyes. Try to picture ONE thing from this book in your mind. What do you see? Can you describe it? (This question makes a link to IDEAS; details help us picture things in our minds.)

√ Do you think this is a book you would like to share with a friend? (This question makes a link to VOICE; writing we love to share is filled with voice.)

WriteTraits®

TEACHER'S GUIDE

Unit 1
Ideas

Overview

This unit focuses on the trait of ideas—the writer's message. This foundational trait includes the main idea plus the details that help support, expand, or clarify that main idea. "Writer's Secrets" at the end of each lesson focus on careful use of conventions to help make meaning clear.

The focus of instruction in this unit will be on
- writing to achieve clarity.
- understanding the concept of "main idea."
- using drawing as a prewriting technique.
- sticking to one topic without wandering.
- understanding the concept of "detail."
- using details to make a main idea more interesting and to create pictures in the reader's mind.

Ideas: *A Definition*

Ideas are all about information. That information can come from a writer's own experience or imagination. When ideas are strong, the writer has a clear message and sticks with the topic. In addition, the writer uses vivid details to paint colorful, interesting pictures in the reader's mind. Pictures can expand ideas for the reader. For this reason, drawing is a highly effective prewriting strategy. However, the message is most clear when writers select their own topics. Several things should be the focus of your instruction: a solid main idea that's easy to identify, interesting details that bring the main idea to life, and clarity.

The Unit at a Glance

The following lessons in the *Teacher's Guide* and practice exercises in the *Student Traitbook* will help develop understanding of the trait of ideas. The Unit Summary provides an opportunity to practice evaluating papers for the trait of ideas.

Unit Introduction: Ideas

Teacher's Guide pages 2–6	The unique features of the trait of ideas are presented along with a rubric and a list of recommended books for teaching the trait of ideas.

Lesson 1: The Word and Picture Team

Teacher's Guide pages 7–9 *Student Traitbook pages 1–5*	In this lesson, students explore the relationship between ideas and pictures.

Lesson 2: What's the BIG Idea?

Teacher's Guide pages 10–12 *Student Traitbook pages 6–9*	Good writing begins with a message. This lesson helps students see the importance of the big, or main, idea.

Lesson 3: Wanted: Good Details!

Teacher's Guide pages 13–15 *Student Traitbook pages 10–13*	This lesson is designed to help students discover the importance of detail in making text both meaningful and appealing.

Lesson 4: Sticking with It

Teacher's Guide pages 16–18 *Student Traitbook pages 14–17*	Students practice identifying text in which the writer wanders, then practice creating a short piece in which the challenge is to stay on topic.

Unit Summary: Ideas

Teacher's Guide page 19 *Overhead numbers 1–4*	Use the student rubric on page 5 and the activities in the Unit Summary to practice assessing writing for the trait of ideas. At the primary level, we strongly encourage the use of verbal descriptors rather than numbers in classroom instruction. If you wish to use numbers to assign classroom grades, 5-point and 6-point rubrics, along with a suggested scoring procedure, appear in the Appendix of this *Teacher's Guide*, pages 201–214.

Teacher Rubric for Ideas

Made it!

This is a strong effort. The writing communicates, writer to reader. It achieves its purpose.

____ The paper has a strong, easy to identify main message.

____ The writer sticks with this main topic and does not try to tell everything.

____ The writer seems to know a lot about his/her topic.

____ The writer consistently chooses interesting details to expand the main idea and hold the reader's attention.

____ The paper is very clear; it is easy to understand what the writer is saying.

Getting there . . .

The paper could clearly be revised, expanded, or clarified, but the good news is, it's on its way! There are many positives.

____ The paper has an identifiable main message.

____ At some point, the writer may introduce one or more unrelated topics.

____ The writer seems to have thought about this topic, though more information would be helpful.

____ The writer shares one or two details; more would expand or clarify the main idea.

____ In most cases, it is possible to figure out what the writer is saying.

It's a start.

The writer has made a start by putting something on paper.

____ The paper does not seem, as yet, to have a main message.

____ The writer does not have enough information or is not sharing enough information to get the message across.

____ The writer does not share details—he/she may share random thoughts or a list that does not relate to any main idea.

____ The writer's point, story, or main message is unclear.

For a rubric with numbers, see the Appendix of this Teacher's Guide, pages 201–214.

Student Rubric for Ideas

Made it!

___ I have a main idea.

___ I stick with my main idea. I do not try to tell about everything.

___ I know a lot about my topic.

___ I share interesting details.

___ It is easy to tell what my paper is about.

Getting there . . .

___ I have a main idea.

___ I stick with my main idea most of the time.

___ I know some things about my topic.

___ I share one or two details.

___ You can guess what my paper is about.

It's a start.

___ I do not have a main message yet.

___ I just wrote the first thing I thought of.

___ I need more information on my topic.

___ I can't think of any details.

___ It is hard to tell what my paper is about.

Recommended Books for Teaching Ideas

Share a whole book, a chapter, a strategy, or a favorite passage. Ask students questions like these: *What do you picture in your mind as you listen? Does the writer have a clear main idea? Do you hear some good details? What does this writer do that you would like to do in your writing?*

Collard, Sneed B. III. 2002. *Leaving Home.* Boston: Houghton. Delightful book about leaving home, written in a leveled style that allows for very simple language or the chance to dip into more complex details when you wish.

Fox, Mem. 1985. *Wilfrid Gordon McDonald Partridge.* La Jolla, CA: Kane/Miller. This classic shows how two vastly different people connect. Examining how memories and personal treasures keep us connected to our past also provides good student prompts.

Kemper, Dave, Ruth Nathan, Patrick Sebranek, and Carol Elsholz. *Write Away* 2002. Wilmington, MA: Great Source. A highly student-friendly handbook that walks students through every step of the writing process.

Muth, Jon J. 2002. *The Three Questions* (based on a story by Leo Tolstoy). New York: Scholastic Press. Nikolai, a young boy, seeks answers to life from a wise old turtle named Leo. This will challenge your students as they look for the main idea.

Pinkney, Sandra L. 2000. *Shades of Black: A Celebration of Our Children.* New York: Scholastic. A reverent and thoughtful look at diversity and detail. *Shades of Black* teaches shades of meaning. Your students may never look at colors casually again.

Simon, Seymour. 2002. *Animals Nobody Loves.* New York: SeaStar Books. Features some of the world's most intriguing but least loved creatures. Text and pictures will fill your students' minds with countless details and prompt enthusiastic writing.

Spandel, Vicki, Ruth Nathan and Laura Robb. *Daybook of Critical Reading and Writing, Grade 2.* 2003. Wilmington, MA: Great Source. Outstanding excerpts from modern literature combine with writing tasks that touch on numerous ideas-related skills.

Waber, Bernard. 2002. *Courage.* Boston: Houghton. Excellent for main ideas as well as for details. An inspirational celebration of the bravery we show in everyday life and how we're all heroes.

The Word and Picture Team

For use with pages 1–5 in the Student Traitbook

Words and pictures work together in writing. Writers often use pictures to expand or clarify information that is difficult to convey with words alone. On the other hand, creating an illustration may prompt a writer's thinking. In this lesson, students explore the "pictures" inside their minds created by vivid text, then practice using pictures as a way of getting into their own writing.

Objectives

Students will gain skill in making mental "pictures" by listening carefully to detailed text. They will also enhance their own writing skills by using drawing as a prewriting strategy.

Skills Focus

- Listening for detail
- Creating a mental image based on that detail
- Sharing ideas with classmates
- Creating a sketch as a prompt for a piece of personal writing
- Creating a short piece of writing to go with the sketch

Time Frame

Allow 15–20 minutes for this lesson, excluding Setting Up the Lesson and any extensions. Students will need time to listen, think, share, sketch, and write, but each step is very short.

Setting Up the Lesson

Read the introduction to Unit 1 to students to help them understand the concept of ideas. Ask students where they think writers get ideas.

In this lesson, you are attempting to connect the power of pictures to writing in that pictures can provide ideas. A good place to start is with a picture book. Choose any favorite, or see the Recommended List of Books for Ideas (page 6 in the Teacher's Guide). Choose one or two pages in which the text and the picture go together especially well. Begin by telling students that in many books, pictures and text go together. Words tell part of the message; the picture tells a part, too. Now, read the text aloud *without showing the picture.* Ask the students, "What did the writer just tell us?" and give them time to summarize what they have heard. Then, show the picture that accompanies the text. Ask, "What does the picture tell us?" Discuss their responses. Remind students that words or pictures may come first.

Teaching the Lesson

Read
Depending on your students, it may be appropriate to read aloud the text in the Student Traitbook. If so, offer a quick reminder about good listening—tuning in with your whole body, using eyes and ears, thinking as you hear each word.

Read or have students read the introduction and the sample passage about Flag from the book *Lost.* Remind students to pay attention to the pictures they "saw" in their minds.

Think
Ask students to share their ideas. What did they see in their minds? Talk about what Flag looked like and what they pictured Flag doing. Did they picture the writer doing anything?

Draw
This activity invites students to draw a picture of any animal they have seen doing something well. This could be a pet or wild animal of any kind at all. Students who want to draw a picture of Flag may do so, but if possible, they should try to think of a new animal from their own experience. Allow a few minutes for drawing.

Write

Ask students to write a few words about the animals in their sketches. There is no length limit for this but (for purposes of building fluency) encourage all students who can to write three sentences or more.

Share

Give students a minute or two to share their pictures and their text with a partner. Remind them to take turns and to listen well. As they share or as soon as they have finished, you may wish to ask, "Did the pictures and the words go together?"

Scribbles Has a Question

Students are asked to be advisors to Scribbles, and they can do this orally. If you read the text together, you will see that today, Scribbles is having difficulty getting started. If students have made the picture-word connection, they might suggest making a sketch or looking at a book with pictures.

A Writer's Secret

Each lesson also includes one writer's secret, offering students practice in one simple conventional strategy that improves clarity. You can do this Writer's Secret activity as part of the lesson or save it for another time. In this lesson, the focus is on the use of capital letters to begin a sentence.

Show them on the overhead or chalkboard how you would like them to make this correction and then ask them to do it. Remind students that a small thing like showing where sentences begin helps make your ideas clear. NOTE: Throughout the program, conventions are presented not just as rules but as a way of making writing clear and easy to read.

Extending the Lesson

- Scribbles forgot capital letters on his sentences. Did any of your students do this as they were writing their animal pieces? Ask them to check!

- Brainstorm a list of things to write about—besides animals. Make a list (three or four ideas are plenty!) on the overhead or chalkboard. Ask students to choose one idea and to follow the same steps used in this lesson.

Advanced Extensions

- Ask students to draft short notes to Scribbles about using pictures with writing.

- During the next week or so, ask students to be on the lookout for samples of writing in which pictures and words team up. Make a collection (you can add to it, too) and discuss the many ways writers use pictures.

Lesson 2

What's the BIG Idea?

For use with pages 6–9 in the Student Traitbook

This lesson is intended to introduce or review the concept of "main idea." In the Student Traitbook, the main idea is compared to a tortilla—it's the big thing that holds all the details together. When a piece of writing is clear, the main idea should be easy to pick out. Details are connected to the main idea and give that idea greater clarity or expanded meaning. Focus and organization both depend on sticking to the main idea. The lack of a main idea is usually a symptom of a bigger problem: e.g., lack of information on the topic.

Objectives

Students will understand the concept of "main idea," gain skill in identifying a main idea in text they hear, and create a short (three sentences plus) piece of writing with a clear main idea.

Skills Focus

- Listening for the main idea in text read aloud
- Identifying the main idea of a passage from among several choices
- Recognizing text that lacks any main idea (because it is a list of small, unconnected ideas)
- Creating a short piece of writing with clear focus

Time Frame

Allow about 20 minutes for this lesson, excluding Setting Up the Lesson and any extensions.

Setting Up the Lesson

Almost everything in the world has parts. One example is a burrito—the sample analogy used in the introduction to this lesson from the Student Traitbook (page 6). Read this introduction together. Then, illustrate it visually. You don't have to use a real burrito—a round piece of cloth will do fine. You can use brown paper bits for meat, green for onions, red for salsa, yellow for cheese, another brown for beans, and so on. As you put it together, talk about the difference between "main idea" and "details." If you can sum up a piece of writing with a word or a phrase or at the most one sentence, it usually means it has a clear main idea. Anything longer probably means that the main idea isn't that clear.

Teaching the Lesson

Read

Read the directions for this section aloud or have students read them silently. Then, share out loud Lisa McCourt's text on polar bear feet, reminding students to listen hard for the main idea: the writer's main (most important) message.

Think

Read the directions together or independently, making sure everyone knows what is expected. Before students make a choice from the list of main ideas, they should answer the question, "Does this writing have a main idea?" Then, give them the chance to work with partners to choose from the four selections.

Ask students to share their responses: How many said "Bears"? How many said "Snowshoes"? Most students should agree on "polar bear feet." If they do not, you may wish to read the passage again and ask them to rethink it. How many times are feet mentioned? (Several!)

Read Again

Read the directions and then share the sample on bike riding, cheddar cheese, and Canada geese. Does this one have a main idea? (No way!)

Share

Students should understand that when a writer shifts gears so many times in one paper, the main idea is lost.

Write

Time to write. First, read the directions aloud. Then, give students time to choose a topic. Encourage them to choose an original topic. If they cannot come up with one, they can choose one from the list. They should put a check mark by the chosen topic, then write three sentences or more about the topic in the space provided. Remember, the main idea of this lesson is "Stick to your main idea!"

When students have finished writing, ask them to go back and read their sentences through. Then, check the right blank. Ask how many checked each blank.

Share

Read the directions aloud. Then, ask for volunteers to share their writing aloud. Two or more students can share. You may wish to share, too! Listen for main ideas as students read and ask your listeners to identify the main idea in each case.

Scribbles Has a Question

Read Scribbles' question aloud. Is this a good idea? Definitely not! This leads to the same kind of problem we heard in the previous paper.

A Writer's Secret

Read A Writer's Secret aloud as students follow along. Then, ask them to look at Scribbles' writing. Did he forget some periods? Yes! How many? Three. Model the way you would like students to insert missing periods. Then, ask them to insert the three missing periods for Scribbles.

Extending the Lesson

- Scribbles forgot some periods in his writing. That makes it hard to tell where sentences stop. Ask students to review their own writing from this lesson. Any missing periods?

Sentences can end in other ways, too, of course. (Model some samples on the overhead or chalkboard.)

- Write a short piece on the overhead or chalkboard in which you write about several things—not sticking to your topic. Ask students to watch and listen closely (read aloud as you write) and to tell you whether your piece has a main idea—or not.

Advanced Extensions

- Read one or more pieces aloud from your classroom literature, asking students to listen carefully. See if they can tell you what the main idea is. Talk about the specific clues that help you identify a main idea. It may be mentioned directly, or the writer may tell things about the main idea.

- Make a main idea "basket," a collection of main ideas written on small pieces of paper or 3 x 5 index cards. Pass it around and ask each person to draw a main idea but not show it to anyone. Then, write short pieces (about three to five sentences) about your main ideas (you write too!) and share some aloud. You can share in small teams or with the whole class. See if you can guess the writer's main idea. If you can, that writer gets a CMI Award: Clear Main Idea.

Wanted: Good Details!

For use with pages 10–13 in the Student Traitbook

Details make pictures in the mind. When details are vivid, the picture springs right to life, all-color, full-animation. In this lesson, students have an opportunity to hear different levels of detail and decide which is most vivid and work at giving a fuzzy piece of writing a detail make-over.

Objectives

Students will choose the most detailed example from among three possibilities and will revise a fuzzy piece of writing to make it more visually appealing for the reader.

Skills Focus

- Listening for detail in writing read aloud
- Choosing (from three possibilities) the sample with the most vivid detail
- Identifying specific details in a piece of written text
- Revising a piece to add detail

Time Frame

Allow 15–20 minutes for this lesson, excluding Setting Up the Lesson and any extensions.

Setting Up the Lesson

To help students see the importance of good details, first read the introduction from the Student Traitbook (page 10) aloud as students follow along. Talk about the differences between the two descriptions of the lost pet. Then, reinforce the contrast by drawing a vague sketch on the overhead. This could be a face, an animal, a butterfly, a plant—anything. Make sure your sketch lacks detail! Now, ask students to help you fill in the details: What kind of eyes? Big! What kind of eyebrows? Bushy! And so on. Draw as they speak. Talk about how their details created a picture—and how details also create pictures in a reader's mind.

Teaching the Lesson

Read

Read the directions aloud. Then, have students read silently or follow along as you read the three passages from *Knights of the Kitchen Table*. Remind them to read or listen for the passage with the best details—picking one will be the next step.

Think

Read the directions aloud. Ask students to think carefully about which of the three choices had the best detail and made the most vivid picture in their minds. Ask them to put a check by #1, #2, or #3. Most should choose #3. Talk about their choices and their reasons.

Think Again

Read the directions aloud. Now, expand students' thinking by asking them to listen again as you read passage #3. Then, ask them to name some specific details the writer uses. Create a list as they mention the details to you. There is space in the *Student Traitbook* (page 11) for them to write along with you if they wish to do so. Try to list at least five details. (There are many more!)

Write

Read the directions aloud as students follow along. When you are sure students understand what to do, read the three sentences aloud again as they listen. Then, have each student choose one sentence to revise. Try to get somewhat even numbers of students to do sentence 1, sentence 2, and sentence 3. Be sure you do one (or all three) as well. Then, invite students to add details to make the picture of the tree more vivid. Remember, each student has only one sentence to revise.

Share

Read the directions aloud. Then, ask a volunteer group of three students to read aloud, sentence by sentence, 1 through 3. The revised version should sound quite different! (You may wish to ask another team of three students to read their revisions aloud also.) A revision might sound something like this: *My favorite climbing tree is two times as tall as our house. It has smooth gray bark. The branches reach out like big arms with leafy fingers.*

Scribbles Has a Question

Read Scribbles' question aloud as students follow along. Then, ask them to write down one question they could ask Scribbles to help him think of some good details about his dog. When students have finished writing, make a list of the questions. Read the list aloud. Remind students to ask themselves questions when they need to add detail.

A Writer's Secret

Make sure everyone knows how and when to use *to, too,* and *two.* Then, read the directions under A Writer's Secret, along with Scribbles' sample sentence. Notice that *to* and *too* are underlined to help students find the words that need changing. Ask if the first *to* is right. No. Ask students to write the version they think is right (*two*). Then, share the right answer. Ask if the second *too* is right. No. Ask students to write the correct version (*to*) and then to share.

Extending the Lesson

• One good way to find a lost pet is with a wanted poster. Invite students to create wanted posters for any pet, real or imaginary. They should draw pictures, then describe the pets, putting as many details as possible into both the pictures and the writing.

• Think of a favorite food—such as pizza. Then, list as many details as you can think of to describe it: how it looks, feels, smells, and tastes. Translate students' details into short sentences on the overhead; then read their detailed masterpiece back to them!

Advanced Extensions

Students have tried revising one sentence. How about three? Invite them to revise this whole piece, adding any details they can think of: *The elephant was big. It was gray. It had a trunk.*

Invite students to write a detailed paragraph (three to five sentences) about one of the following topics— or any topic of their own:

_____ Something I saw at the zoo

_____ A food I do not like

_____ Wild weather!

_____ My own topic: _____

Suggest that they list a few details before writing. That way, they will not leave out anything important!

Sticking with It

For use with pages 14–17 in the Student Traitbook

Sometimes students will tell you they have nothing to write about. The truth is, there's almost *too* much to write about! Some writers try to take on all the topics they can think of in one piece, and the result is a jumble. This lesson builds on the concepts introduced in Lesson 2: What's the BIG Idea? It is designed to help students see the importance of staying on track and not trying to tell about two— or three—things at the same time.

Objectives

Students learn to distinguish between writing that sticks with the topic and writing that does not and to create a short piece that focuses on one selected topic.

Skills Focus

- Listening for writing that sticks with one topic
- Distinguishing between writing that wanders and writing that does not
- Creating a short original piece that sticks with one topic

Time Frame

Allow 15–20 minutes for this lesson, excluding Setting Up the Lesson and any extensions.

Setting Up the Lesson

Sticking with one topic can be hard, especially if you have a lot to say about a lot of things. Writers need to make choices, though, or their writing can become chaotic. You can illustrate this orally. Tell students you would like to tell them about your weekend. Start with one story, then switch gears, then switch again—and see if anyone notices: e.g., *Last weekend I played with my family in the snow. Something really funny happened! Next summer I am going to plant a garden. Did you know baby lions actually have spots?*

Ask if they noticed anything funny about your weekend story. You may need to coax them a bit, but if your variations are drastic enough, most of them should notice it! Ask what happens when someone talks like this. Writing works the same way. It is important for the writer to stick with it!

Teaching the Lesson

Read

Read the directions aloud or have students read them silently. Then, share Sample 1 and Sample 2 aloud, pausing after each one to let students decide if the writer stuck with the topic—or wandered. When students have finished marking choices, discuss their responses. Most should hear the wandering in the first sample, while Sample 2 sticks with the topic.

Think

This section requires students to get specific about any wandering they noticed in Sample 1. Read the directions aloud. Make sure everyone has a pencil. Then, return to Sample 1. Read the sample aloud if you feel it will be helpful, reminding students to underline anything that wanders.

Share

Read the directions aloud. Then, ask a few students to share what they underlined. They should have underlined all of the last three sentences, which have nothing to do with the farm.

Think

Read the directions aloud. Then, invite students to choose a topic from the list or to come up with one of their own. They need to know enough about the topic so that they will not be tempted to wander! They should also take a minute to think about what they want to say—for the next step will be to write.

Write

Read the directions aloud. Then, ask students to write at least three sentences about their topics in the space provided. Remind them to stick with the topic.

Share

Read the directions under Share. Invite students to share with a partner. Partners should listen carefully and try to notice if each paper sticks with the topic. After sharing, students should look at their papers carefully, and if they did wander, put a star ☆ by that spot.

Scribbles Has a Question

Read Scribbles' question aloud and ask students to write their opinions. Notice that Scribbles wants to write about everything. Student advisors should discourage this!

A Writer's Secret

Read the text from A Writer's Secret aloud. Ask students to notice the difference between Scribbles' sentence (I **lick** snakes) and the corrected version (I **like** snakes). Talk about how this tiny difference changes the meaning. Then, ask students to look carefully at the last sentence. Do not read it aloud. Just let them look. If they have trouble finding the mistake, ask them to work with a partner. See if they can guess which word is wrong. Then, see if they can guess how to fix it. Share the correct answer: *It is time to leave **for** school.*

Extending the Lesson

- Look back at the sample from Sample 1 about the farm. It begins to wander with the sentence "I am good at math" and it never comes back. What other things could the author write about that would "stick with" the topic of the farm? See if you can come up with two more "stick with it" sentences. Then, read your class revision aloud.

- Write a short piece (4 or 5 sentences) in which one sentence (or more) wanders from the topic. Read your piece aloud to students and ask them to help you identify the place where you wandered from your main topic.

Advanced Extensions

- Having a strong main idea helps keep a writer from wandering. Look back at Sample 1. See if you can identify this writer's main idea: *The farm is fun.* Look at Sample 2. Identify the writer's main idea: *Nico and I did a bubble project.*

- Try identifying the main idea in some other pieces of writing. Pull a short article from the newspaper. Read an advertisement aloud. Try a recipe or a short paragraph from the encyclopedia. Do any of these samples wander? Probably not. The stronger the main idea, the less likely it is the writer will wander.

Ideas

Teacher's Guide pages 5, 118–132
Overhead numbers 1–4

Objective

Students will review and apply what they have learned about the trait of ideas.

Reviewing Ideas

Review with students what they have learned about the trait of ideas. Ask students to discuss what ideas are and to explain why ideas are important in a piece of writing. Then, ask them to recall the main points about ideas that are discussed in Unit 1. Students' responses should include the following points:

- Get ideas from pictures.
- Write about only one main idea.
- Use details to make your writing clear.
- Stick to one main idea.

Applying Ideas

To help students apply what they have learned about the trait of ideas, distribute copies of the Student Rubric for Ideas on page 5 of this Teacher's Guide. Students will use these to rate one or more of the sample papers that begin on page 114. The papers for ideas are also on the overhead transparencies 1–4.

Before students look at the papers, explain that a rubric will help them determine how strong a piece of writing is for a particular trait. Preview the Student Rubric for Ideas, pointing out that a paper very strong in ideas is rated as "Made it!" and a paper very weak in ideas is rated as "It's a start." Tell students to read the rubric and then read the paper they will rate. Then, tell them to look at the paper and the rubric together to determine the rating the paper should receive. Encourage students to make notes on each paper to help them evaluate it. For example, they might put an X next to details unrelated to the main idea.

Organization

Overview

This unit focuses on organization—putting information into an order that makes sense. It builds on skills developed through Unit 1: Ideas. Organization is about staying on track, sharing details in an order that is easy to follow, and beginning and ending a piece effectively. As you will see in going through the unit, the traits of ideas and organization are closely connected.

The focus of instruction in this unit will be
- putting details in an order that makes sense.
- writing a lead that gets a paper off to a strong start.
- telling one story at a time.
- finishing a paper with a strong conclusion.

Organization: *A Definition*

Organization is the internal structure in a piece of writing. Like the skeleton of an animal, it holds everything together. Strong organization gives ideas direction, purpose, and momentum, guiding the reader skillfully from point to point. When organization is strong, details work together to form a clear picture. Several things make organization effective, and you should focus on these things in your instruction: an organizational sequence that makes ideas easy to follow, a clear and sustained focus on the main idea, a compelling lead that pulls the reader in, and an appropriate conclusion that makes a piece of writing feel finished.

The Unit at a Glance

The following lessons in the *Teacher's Guide* and practice exercises in the *Student Traitbook* will help develop understanding of the trait of organization. The Unit Summary provides an opportunity to practice evaluating papers for the trait of organization.

Unit Introduction: Organization

Teacher's Guide pages 20–24	The unique features of the trait of organization are presented along with a rubric and a list of recommended books for teaching the trait of organization.

Lesson 5: Just like a Puzzle

Teacher's Guide pages 25–27 *Student Traitbook pages 18–22*	When details within a piece of writing fit together well, the main idea stands out.

Lesson 6: Starting Off with a Bang!

Teacher's Guide pages 28–30 *Student Traitbook pages 23–26*	A good lead gets a piece of writing off to a good start. This lesson gives students an opportunity to rate leads as strong or weak and to try writing an effective lead on a selected topic.

Lesson 7: One Story at a Time!

Teacher's Guide pages 31–33 *Student Traitbook pages 27–30*	This lesson builds upon Lesson 4, Sticking with It, by encouraging students to write on a single main topic at a time.

Lesson 8: The Finish Line

Teacher's Guide pages 34–36 *Student Traitbook pages 31–34*	Students compare various endings, choose favorites, and try their hands at writing an ending to a short story.

Unit Summary: Organization

Teacher's Guide page 37 *Overhead numbers 5–8*	Use the Student Rubric for Organization on page 23 and the activities in the Unit Summary to practice assessing writing for the trait of organization. If you wish to use numbers to assign classroom grades, 5-point and 6-point primary rubrics for teachers, along with a suggested scoring procedure, appear in the Appendix of this *Teacher's Guide*, pages 201–214.

© Great Source. Copying is prohibited.

Teacher Rubric for Organization

Made it!

This is a strong effort. The writing is very easy to follow.
It achieves its purpose.

_____ The paper has a strong, logical sense of order. It is easy to follow.

_____ The writer sticks to the main idea; he/she does not meander.

_____ The beginning (lead) is compelling and draws the reader in.

_____ The ending fits the paper well and makes it feel finished.

Getting there . . .

The organization could use some tidying up or the lead/conclusion
could be stronger. The good news is, the paper is on its way! There
are many positives.

_____ The paper has a reasonable sense of order; some details could be moved or eliminated altogether.

_____ Much of the time, the writer sticks to the main idea, but now and then he/she meanders down a side trail.

_____ The paper has a beginning.

_____ The paper has an ending.

It's a start.

The writer has made a start by putting something on paper.

_____ Details seem random or out of order; lack of a main idea could be the root cause.

_____ The writer meanders or tries to present two stories/ideas at the same time.

_____ The paper does not have any real beginning; it just starts in.

_____ The paper does not have any real ending; it just stops.

For a rubric with numbers, see the Appendix of this Teacher's Guide, pages 201–214.

Student Rubric for Organization

Made it!

___ Everything is in order.

___ I stick to my main idea.

___ My paper gets off to a great start!

___ My paper has a strong ending. It feels finished.

Getting there . . .

___ Parts of my paper are in order.

___ Sometimes, I wander!

___ I have a beginning. It is one I have used before.

___ I have an ending. It is one I have used before.

It's a start.

___ My paper is out of order.

___ I wander a lot. I try to tell about too many things.

___ My paper does not have a beginning. I just started to write.

___ My paper is not finished. I just stopped. Or, I wrote the end.

Recommended Books for Teaching Organization

As you share literature, ask students questions like these: *Is this piece easy to follow? Do all the "puzzle pieces" seem to fit in the right spots? Can you get the big picture from the way the writer organized things? Did you like this lead/ending? What did this writer do that you would like to do in your writing?*

Ada, Alma Flor. 2002. *I Love Saturdays y domingos*. New York: Simon & Schuster. A book of comparisons, featuring languages, grandparents, and cultures.

Collard, Sneed B. III. 2002. *Beaks!* Watertown, MA: Charlesbridge. Excellent nonfiction text that illustrates the power of starting with a small topic and sticking with it.

Curtis, Jamie Lee. 1993. *When I Was Little*. New York: HarperCollins. Whimsical, lighthearted illustration of comparison organization.

Cuyler, Margery. 1991. *That's Good! That's Bad!* New York: Holt. A classic tale of a little boy whose visit to the zoo is only the beginning of a wild adventure.

Fleming, Denise. 1997. *Time to Sleep*. New York: Holt. A simple but appealing tale of how animals prepare for their winter's sleep. Easy-to-imitate organizational structure.

Fox, Mem. 1989. *Night Noises*. San Diego: Harcourt Brace. Tale of 90-year-old Lily Laceby and her dog. Great for predicting/anticipating and coming up with an ending!

Gill, Shelley. 1990. *Alaska's Three Bears*. Seattle, WA: Sasquatch Books. Adaptation of the traditional "Three Bears" story. Students can follow the underlying pattern as each bear finds its native home.

Kemper, Dave, Ruth Nathan, Patrick Sebranek, and Carol Elsholz. *Write Away*. 2001. Wilmington, MA: Great Source. A highly student-friendly handbook that walks students through every step of the writing process.

Marshall, James. 1975. *The Guest*. New York: Houghton Mifflin. Strong lead and ending provide good models for children to emulate.

Spandel, Vicki, Ruth Nathan and Laura Robb. *Daybook of Critical Reading and Writing, Grade 2*. 2003. Wilmington, MA: Great Source. Outstanding excerpts from the best of modern literature (nonfiction to poetry) combine with writing tasks that touch on numerous organization-related skills.

Walsh, Melanie. 2002. *My Beak, Your Beak*. Boston: Houghton Mifflin. Excellent for exploring comparison-contrast organization with young thinkers.

Lesson 5

Just like a Puzzle

For use with pages 18–22 in the Student Traitbook

Put a puzzle together in random order, and you'd wind up with a very odd picture indeed! Writing is like that, too. If you want main ideas to stand out clearly— to create a picture in the reader's mind—you need to put the puzzle pieces in the right order.

Objectives

Students will sharpen their listening skills by identifying writing that has strong (or weak) order and will enhance their own organizational skills by working on an out-of-order piece.

Skills Focus

- Listening to samples of strong or weak organization
- Discussing strong versus weak organization
- Identifying (by listening) a piece that has strong organization
- Reorganizing a recipe in which the steps are out of order

Time Frame

Allow about 20 minutes for this lesson, excluding Setting Up the Lesson and any extensions. Students will need time to listen, think, share, and reorder, but each step is short.

Setting Up the Lesson

Introduce the trait of organization by reading and talking about page 18 of the Student Traitbook. Conclude that order and organization are important in writing. This lesson is about organizing bits of information—or individual sentences—as if they were pieces in a puzzle. You can illustrate this perfectly with a small, simple jigsaw puzzle. This should be a puzzle you have already put together yourself, but one your students have not seen before. Begin by talking about how one piece of the puzzle does not tell much. Hold up one piece and invite students to guess what the "big picture" might be. Then, talk about how the picture comes together once all the pieces are in place. Talk about how writing is like a puzzle—all the pieces need to fit.

Teaching the Lesson

Read

Read aloud or have students read silently Sample #1, then pause for students' responses. Remind them to listen to the organization. Make sure you have read the sample yourself, so you are prepared for its lack of organization and for the discussion to follow. Do the pieces fit? (No!)

Think

Pause to let students respond to Sample #1. They should put an X in the blank that matches their reactions. Most should agree that the writing is hopelessly out of order. Talk about their responses. Ask how many felt each way and why.

Read Again

This time, you'll be sharing Sample #2. All the pieces have been put in order. Read Sample #2 aloud as students follow along. Remind them to listen for the organization. Are the pieces in order this time? (Yes!)

Think

Ask students to mark their responses with an X in the right blank: *This is much better* or *It was better the first time.* Most should agree that it is improved. Discuss results.

Read

Students will now stretch their organizing skills by working on a short, five-step recipe. The five steps are out of order, and it is their job to put them back in order. You can do this lesson two ways: one is to ask students to put a number in each blank to show how the steps should go, 1–5. The second is to make copies of the recipe in the Student Traitbook, pass them out, and ask students to cut them into strips. If you do it the second way, students can work in teams of two or three, so you will only need one copy for each two to three students.

Share

Remind students to read the "final" recipe out loud to themselves when they are done.

It is now time for you to share the steps in the right order. You may wish to pause after each step to see how many students are still with you. Here is the right order:

1. With an adult's help, cut some celery into six pieces.

2. Spread some peanut butter on top of each celery "log."

3. Place raisin "ants" in the peanut butter on top of your celery "log."

4. Put your "logs" on a small plate.

5. Enjoy your tasty snack!

Scribbles Has a Question

Scribbles is asking if it is OK to write things in any order. It is sometimes all right to do this if you are writing in a personal journal, but when you are writing for a reader, order is important. This is the concept students should express in their notes to Scribbles.

A Writer's Secret

Ask if Scribbles forgot today's Writer's Secret. (Yes!) How many question marks are missing? (Two.) Show students on the chalkboard or an overhead how you would like them to mark text to insert a question mark. They should insert question marks after the first and third sentences.

Extending the Lesson

- Invite students to create a short recipe or other how-to piece of their own. The writing should have three to five steps. Remind them to read the steps out loud when they are finished to make sure the order makes sense.

- Invite students to try another organizational pattern—such as compare-contrast. You will find some excellent models for this in the list of Recommended Books for Teaching Organization (page 24 of this Teacher's Guide).

Advanced Extensions

- Ask students to write a simple set of directions or a simple recipe of three to five steps. Then, invite them to rewrite it, only this time with one or more steps *out of order*. Trade with partners, and see if the partners can "put the puzzle back together."

- Numbering can help organize other kinds of writing, too. Ask students to list three to five things about a chosen topic. Or they can list three to five events that happen in a fictional story. Then write. How does a list help a writer keep organized?

Lesson 6

Starting Off with a Bang!

For use with pages 23–26 in the Student Traitbook

In writing, it's important to get off to a good start. This lesson gives students a chance to explore the concept of a strong lead. If the lead is flat, odds are the reader may find something else to do and never even get to the main point!

Objectives

In this lesson, students develop an understanding of the concept of "lead" and begin to differentiate between strong leads and those that are less effective in getting a reader's attention.

Skills Focus

- Understanding the concept of "lead"
- Discussing some things a good lead can do
- Use listening skills to distinguish between strong and weak leads
- Practice creating an original lead for a self-selected topic
- Sharing and discussing leads with partners

Time Frame

Allow about 20 minutes for this lesson, excluding Setting Up the Lesson and any extensions.

© Great Source. Copying is prohibited.

Setting Up the Lesson

You need a small ramp (about three feet long) and a small rubber ball for this demonstration. You can set it up on a desk, table, or the floor. Roll the ball very gently toward the ramp—making sure you do not give it enough oomph to make it to the top. Let students know you feel very disappointed your ball didn't make it! Try another roll—but again, make sure your ball doesn't quite make it. Ask what is wrong. By now they should be flooding you with advice to try harder! Of course, you will succeed. Talk about how you need some power, some energy, to get your ball going. Writers need energy at the beginning of a piece of writing, too. Otherwise, the writing gets off to a weak start!

Read the introduction aloud, and remind students that the beginning of a piece of writing is called the lead. Ask if anyone can guess why. Let them know that a lead "leads" readers right into the writing. That's why it has to be energetic and appealing!

Teaching the Lesson

Read

Read the directions aloud as students follow along. Pay particular attention to the things leads can do. If you like, share one or two leads with students from the literature in your classroom (See the Recommended Books for Teaching Organization list, page 24 of this Teacher's Guide for ideas). Ask for their responses to each lead. Does it get their attention? Does it make them feel like reading more? If so, good! That's the sign of a strong lead.

Now, explain that you will read four leads from the lesson out loud. Pause after each one to get students' reactions. They will mark their responses to the question "Would you like to hear more?" with an X in the space provided.

Discuss students' responses. Which leads did they like best? Most should agree that the first and last leads were strong, while leads 2 and 3 were fairly uninteresting. Remind students that good writers need to think like readers sometimes. Paying attention to what you like as a reader helps you to be a strong writer.

Think and Share

Ask students to read the directions, then finish the sentence "A good lead..." Share some responses aloud. Add your thoughts, too.

Write

Ask students to read the directions under Write, then to choose a topic (encourage them to come up with a personal topic, if possible). When they have chosen a topic, they should write a lead that invites the reader in. Remind them what a good lead is supposed to do—lead the reader into the writing. Also, remind them that a lead is short. It is not the whole paper!

Share

Invite two or three students to share their leads, and talk about them. Try to identify what each lead does that works well. Look for differences in leads—you do not want them to all sound alike. Share your own lead, too.

Scribbles Has a Question

Read the text as students follow along. Then, briefly discuss ways to solve Scribbles' problem—not being able to think of a good lead. Talk about what a good lead does and possible ways Scribbles could begin.

A Writer's Secret

First, show students how to write a symbol # to indicate the need to insert space. Have everyone try writing this symbol. Explain that this is a handy symbol to use if you forget a space and run two words together. Show students on the overhead or chalkboard how to use this symbol.

Now, read the directions as students follow along. Stop when you get to Scribbles' sentence. See if students can read this on their own. Ask if they can find places where Scribbles forgot spaces. (Yes.) How many? (Three.) Ask them to mark those spots using the right symbol.

Extending the Lesson

- Go back to the leads students wrote. Ask them to finish the piece of writing by adding two to four more sentences. Does a good lead help a writer stay on the topic? (Yes!)

- Make a classroom poster on leads. Write down three to five things a good lead can do. Post it where everyone can see it.

Advanced Extensions

- Ask students to look at any piece of writing they have been working on. Does it have a lead? Ask them to underline it. Then, ask them to try writing it another way. They should use their imaginations! Which lead do they like better?

- Ask students to look through literature in your classroom or library for good leads. Each student should find one or two. Have a "lead-fest" and read as many aloud as you have time for. Identify some favorites.

One Story at a Time!

For use with pages 27–30 in the Student Traitbook

Trying to consume a big turkey dinner and a steak dinner at one meal would be too much for most eaters. Readers don't like to be overwhelmed, either. A good way to lose focus in any piece of writing is to try writing about two topics at the same time. Many writers do this. They let another topic or story sneak into the writing, making it difficult to figure out the writer's main point. Good organization demands staying on track, and that means sticking with one topic or story.

Objectives

Students will recognize the importance of telling one story or sticking with one topic in order to keep the focus strong.

Skills Focus

- Using listening skills to determine when a writer is telling *two* stories—not one
- Identifying specific sentences that are off the writer's intended topic
- Creating an original piece of writing that focuses on one topic
- Sharing and discussing writing with a partner

Time Frame

Allow about 20 minutes for this lesson, excluding Setting Up the Lesson and any extensions.

Setting Up the Lesson

One of the best ways to draw students' attention to a writing problem is to model it. Do that. First, pick a topic on which you could write three to five sentences. Then, think of another topic that might "sneak into your writing" as you go! Begin writing on the first topic on the overhead or chalkboard. Give your writing a title, and make sure the title fits the first topic. Make the print big and read aloud as you go. When you have written three or four sentences, completely switch topics. See if your students notice. If they do not say anything, write two or three short sentences on this different "sneaky" topic. Then, read the whole piece aloud. Ask if students notice anything funny about your writing. If they still do not notice, ask if you changed topics. Where? Provide as many clues as you need to until they can spot the place you went off-track. Explain that when writers stick with one topic or story, readers do not get confused.

Teaching the Lesson

Read

Ask students to read the directions on page 27 of the Student Book. Provide help as you need to. When they are ready, read the short passage called "My Pirate Birthday Party" aloud.

Think

Ask students to follow along as you read the directions before the list. Make sure everyone has access to a blue crayon and a red crayon. Then, give them time to mark their lists for "My Pirate Birthday Party." The first four items should be *red*; the remaining sentences should all be *blue*. Discuss this. How many students noticed that the sentences about the dog Cody had nothing to do with the birthday party? Ask what this writer should do. (Save the story about Cody for another paper.)

Think & Pick

Ask students to read the directions under Think & Pick, then to choose a topic from the list. Encourage students to come up with an original topic, if possible. If they cannot think of something, they can choose one of our topics. Ask them to write their chosen topics in the space provided. Then, they should think about the writer's question, "What do I want to say about this topic?"

Write

Ask students to read the directions. What are the important things to remember? Write at least three sentences. Stay with one topic or one story! Don't let other topics or stories sneak in!

Share

Ask students to read the directions. Then, they should share their stories with a partner and decide together if they stayed on the topic. Those who did should put a red star (with a crayon) at the top of their papers.

Scribbles Has a Question

Read the text under Scribbles Has a Question aloud as students follow along. What are his two topics? (Going to the beach and a storm.) Should he write about both? What will happen if he does? Ask students to write their thoughts in a short note to Scribbles.

A Writer's Secret

Titles are important. Like every "piece of the puzzle," the title needs to fit. A good title can help a writer stay focused, too. Read the directions and Scribbles' short story aloud as students follow along. Together, brainstorm some possible titles for Scribbles' story. Talk about the idea of coming up with a title last.

Extending the Lesson

- Look again at the copy for "My Pirate Birthday Party." What does the writer's title tell us? What did the writer want this story to be about?
- Read a story aloud without sharing the title. Ask students to tell you the writer's main idea. Then, brainstorm possible titles for the story. Write some down. Then, share the author's original title. Do students like the author's original? Or do they like one of their own better?

Advanced Extensions

- Ask students to look at a piece of writing they are working on (or recently worked on). Does the title fit? Does everything in the paper go with the title? If not, this could be a good time to revise by doing one or more of these things:

1. Cross out sentences that do not go with the title

2. Add one sentence that does go with the title

3. Change the title so it fits!

- Sometimes, two ideas can go together. For example, maybe there is also a way for the writer of "My Pirate Birthday Party" to write about Cody the dog. What would the writer need to do? Answer: Show how the ideas connect or go together. This can be a difficult concept for students to grasp. You can offer some examples, though—perhaps Cody steals a piece of cake or kids play games with Cody at the party. That way, the focus is still on the birthday party. If students seem to understand this concept of connecting two ideas, try having them write just one sentence about Cody that would link the dog and the party. See if they can make the link! This is an advanced skill. If your students can do it, celebrate!

The Finish Line

For use with pages 31–34 in the Student Traitbook

Arguably the two most important parts in any piece of writing are the beginning and ending. In Lesson 6: Starting Off with a Bang!, students explored the value and impact of a strong lead. Now, they put the "other bookend" in place by looking at endings. A good ending is more than the words "The End." It makes a piece of writing feel finished.

Objectives

Students will understand the concept of ending as a way of finishing the writing and begin to explore some options for writing a strong conclusion.

Skills Focus

- Understanding the concept of *ending*
- Discussing and thinking about some characteristics of a good ending
- Using listening skills to identify strong endings
- Choosing the best ending to a story from three possibilities
- Creating an original ending for an existing, unfinished story

Time Frame

Allow about 20 minutes for this lesson, excluding Setting Up the Lesson and any extensions.

Setting Up the Lesson

Identify an interesting paragraph you think your students might like to hear (a piece you can read aloud in under three minutes). A poem works well for this activity, too. Tell them you are going to share it out loud. Start, and then stop abruptly in the middle and calmly close the book. You can even stop in the middle of a sentence. See if students notice your sudden stop. They should, if you're dramatic enough! Ask how it feels to stop in the middle. Most should say it feels strange—it feels . . . unfinished! Read the Introduction as students follow along. Talk about how a good ending is more than just the words "The End." It needs to satisfy the reader.

Teaching the Lesson

Read

How do pieces of writing end? Read aloud the text under Read as students follow along. Take your time with the list of possible things endings can do. See if anyone has anything to add to this list. Then, tell students you will be sharing two endings, and they will have a chance to show how much they like each one by marking the right comment with an X. Read Ending #1 and Ending #2, pausing after each to let students respond.

Read and Choose

Share the directions under Read and Choose as students follow along. Tell them that this time they will be choosing just one of the endings from three possibilities. They should choose the one they like best after they hear all three. Now, read aloud the three endings, A, B, and C, or have students read them silently.

When students have finished reading or listening, ask them which ending they liked best and why. Don't be afraid to share your own thoughts once they have shared theirs. Ending A provides a clear image of Sonny wanting to get out of the barn, then taking off. This works well because it leaves the reader thinking and wondering about another possible story to come. Ending B ends with a sentence we don't need: "That's all there is to tell." Ending C includes the words "The End," which are not needed. Writers do not need to announce their endings.

Write

Read the directions aloud as students follow along. Pause to be sure everyone understands the activity: to write an ending to this unfinished story. Now, read the story aloud as students follow along. Then, give students time to write their endings.

When everyone has finished, invite two or three students to share their endings aloud with the class. Did everyone find a different way to end the story? Talk about how stories can end in different ways. Share your ending too, if you like!

Scribbles Has a Question

Read the text aloud as students follow along. Then, talk about Scribbles' problem. What's wrong with just saying "The End"? How do you usually end your day with your students? Do you sum up things you have done? Give students reminders? Talk about what's coming up tomorrow? What if you just said "The End"? Would that be an odd way to wrap up your day?

A Writer's Secret

Show students that they should mark a capital "I" in text. They might just write the capital over the lower case letter. Or, you might have them use a copy editor's symbol of three small lines under the letter, like this: i̲

Then, read the text under A Writer's Secret aloud, up to Scribbles' sentence. Stop at that point. Let students read Scribbles' writing on their own. Ask if Scribbles forgot today's Writer's Secret. (Yes.) How many I's did Scribbles miss? (Three.) Ask students to correct them now as you showed them.

Extending the Lesson

• Choose a book with a good ending. Read it aloud to students, but do not read the ending. Talk about ending possibilities. What might happen?

Make a list. Then, share the author's ending and compare it to your students' versions. Which one do they like best? Did anyone anticipate the author's actual ending?

• As you share books during the coming week or two, talk about the ending to each one. Keep track of favorites. If time permits, write out favorite endings and post them. Read them again at some point to remind students of their favorites.

Advanced Extensions

• Write a short story or essay on the overhead (three or four sentences will do) and omit the ending. Ask students to help you come up with an ending that fits. If they come up with more than one idea, write down several possibilities, and as a class, choose your favorite. Talk about why you like it.

• Ask students to look at their endings from a recent piece of their own writing. Do their endings sound more like A, B, or C from the lesson? See if they can add one image or one detail to make the ending stronger than before. They can also revise by eliminating the words "The End" or the sentence "That is the end of my story." Those aren't needed.

Organization

Teacher's Guide pages 23, 133–145
Overhead numbers 5–8

Objective

Students will review and apply what they have learned about the trait of organization.

Reviewing Organization

Review with students what they have learned about the trait of organization. Ask students to discuss what organization means and to explain why it is important in a piece of writing. Then, ask them to recall the main points about organization that are discussed in Unit 2. Students' responses should include the following points:

- Write a strong lead.
- Put details in order.
- Tell one story at a time.
- Write a strong ending.

Applying Organization

To help students apply what they have learned about the trait of organization, distribute copies of the Student Rubric for Organization on page 23 of this Teacher's Guide. Students will use these to rate one or more of the sample papers that begin on page 114. The papers for organization are also on the overhead transparencies 5–8.

Before students look at the papers, explain that a rubric will help them determine how strong a piece of writing is for a particular trait. Preview the Student Rubric for Organization, pointing out that a paper very strong in organization is rated as "Made it!" and a paper very weak in organization is rated as "It's a start." Tell students to read the rubric and then read the paper they will rate. Then, tell them to look at the paper and the rubric together to determine the rating the paper should receive. Encourage students to make notes on each paper to help them evaluate it. For example, they might count how many stories they are telling at the same time.

Unit 3
Voice

Overview

This unit focuses on voice, a trait that reflects individuality, honesty, and expression. Students who choose their own topics, care about their topics, and express their real feelings have stronger voice. In addition, students who write to an audience have stronger voice. As they hear the voices of other writers, they develop a strong sense of what voice is, and they may even "try on" the voice of a writer they like.

The focus of instruction in this unit will be

- helping students listen for the presence of voice in writing read aloud.
- giving students practice in coming up with their own words to describe voice.
- choosing personal topics to help students let their own voices "roar."
- using very simple revision techniques to build voice into flat writing.

Voice: *A Definition*

Voice is what keeps readers reading. As one teacher put it, ideas are what you have to say; voice is how you say it. Some elements of voice—such as personality or honesty—need to be nurtured (through modeling and positive comments). Other elements, however, can be taught through use of detail or lively language and choice of personally important topics. Voice is also a reflection of confidence. When a writer does not know a topic well, it is good to gain information first and then write. Young writers should also know that even tiny changes, such as adding one descriptive word or making an honest comment, can do wonders to infuse writing with voice.

The Unit at a Glance

The following lessons in the *Teacher's Guide* and practice exercises in the *Student Traitbook* will help develop understanding of the trait of voice. The Unit Summary provides an opportunity to practice evaluating papers for the trait of voice.

Unit Introduction: Voice

Teacher's Guide pages 38–42

The unique features of the trait of voice are presented along with a rubric and a list of recommended literature for teaching voice.

Lesson 9: An Ear for Voice

Teacher's Guide pages 43–45
Student Traitbook pages 35–39

Students explore the voices of other writers, comparing them for voice and beginning to work on a personal definition of "voice."

Lesson 10: A Bouquet of Voices

Teacher's Guide pages 46–48
Student Traitbook pages 40–43

Students listen to three distinct voices and brainstorm words to describe each one.

Lesson 11: Hear Me Roar!

Teacher's Guide pages 49–51
Student Traitbook pages 44–47

In this lesson, students select a personally important topic, then use both drawing and writing to express their individual voices.

Lesson 12: More Voice, Please!

Teacher's Guide pages 52–54
Student Traitbook pages 48–51

In this lesson, students are introduced to several ways of putting voice into lifeless writing.

Unit Summary: Voice

Teacher's Guide page 55
Overhead numbers 9–12

Use the student rubric on page 41 and the activities in the Summary to practice assessing writing for the trait of voice. At the primary level, we strongly encourage the use of verbal descriptors rather than numbers. The recommended rubrics are designed to support this philosophy. (For those who wish to use numbers for purposes of assigning classroom grades, 5-point and 6-point primary rubrics for teachers, along with a suggested scoring procedure, appear in the Appendix of this *Teacher's Guide*, pages 201–214.)

Teacher Rubric for Voice

Made it!

This is a strong effort. The writing displays life, energy, enthusiasm, confidence, and individuality.

_____ This is a piece you will want to share aloud.

_____ The writing sounds like this writer and no other; it's individual.

_____ The writing is consistently lively, expressive, engaging, and heartfelt.

_____ The paper shows feelings; the writer seems to care about the topic and to speak right to the audience.

Getting there . . .

The writing displays moments of voice. It's on its way!

_____ There are moments you might share aloud.

_____ Here and there the writer's individual voice peeks through.

_____ There is at least a sentence, a word, or a phrase that stands out; it's lively and expressive—striking or different.

_____ At least one sentence shows engagement with the topic or sensitivity to the audience.

It's a start.

The writer has made a start by putting something on paper.

_____ This paper is not ready to be shared aloud—yet!

_____ It's hard to connect this writing with a particular writer.

_____ The writer has not put enough of him- or herself into the writing (yet) to make it lively and expressive.

_____ The paper does not reflect any engagement with the topic or audience—yet!

For a rubric with numbers, see the Appendix of this Teacher's Guide, pages 201–214.

Student Rubric for Voice

Made it!

_____ I love how my paper sounds.

_____ This sounds like me.

_____ My paper is lively. I say what I really think and feel.

_____ My paper shows feelings.

Getting there . . .

_____ I like my paper. It sounds ok.

_____ Parts of it sound like me.

_____ Some parts are lively. I share my real feelings at least once.

_____ At least one sentence shows feelings.

It's a start.

_____ I am not sure I like it.

_____ I do not think it sounds like me.

_____ My paper is not lively. I did not share my real feelings.

_____ My paper does not show feelings—yet!

Recommended Books for Teaching Voice

Read as you'd like to hear your students read—with expression and life. Ask students questions like these: *Do you hear voice in this piece of writing? Or does it leave you hungry for more? How would you describe this voice? Do you think this writer is sharing his or her real feelings? What things does this writer do to put voice into his/her writing?*

Blake, Robert J. 2002. *Togo*. New York: Philomel Books. Retracing the journey that Togo undertook in 1925 to bring life-saving serum to Nome, Alaska.

Byars, Betsy. 2000. *Me Tarzan*. New York: HarperCollins. A funny and engaging chapter book about Dorothy's struggles to become Tarzan in the school play.

Dahl, Roald. 1980. *The Twits*. New York: Puffin Books. Razor-sharp humor and outrageous pranks combine with rollicking adventure in one of Dahl's most loved books.

George, Twig C. 2000. *Jellies*. Brookfield, CT: Millbrook Press Inc. Expressive, lively text illustrates the power of voice to bring nonfiction text to life.

Haseley, Dennis. 2002. *A Story for Bear*. New York: Harcourt, Inc. A moving and enchanting tale of a bear who becomes entranced by a woman's read-aloud voice.

Kemper, Dave, Ruth Nathan, Patrick Sebranek, and Carol Elsholz. *Write Away*. 2001. Wilmington, MA: Great Source. A highly student-friendly handbook that walks students through every step of the writing process.

Spandel, Vicki, Ruth Nathan and Laura Robb. *Daybook of Critical Reading and Writing, Grade 2*. 2003. Wilmington, MA: Great Source. Outstanding excerpts from the best of modern literature combine with writing tasks that enhance voice by asking young writers to share thoughts and opinions while building fluency.

Stock, Catherine. 2001. *Gugu's House*. New York: Houghton Mifflin. Set in the plains of Zimbabwe about a girl and her grandmother as they face the challenges of nature.

White, E. B. 1980. *Charlotte's Web*. New York: HarperCollins. E. B. White's beloved tale about Wilbur, Charlotte, and Fern. Countless passages illustrate how passion, vivid detail and imagery, and dialogue feed voice in writing.

More Ideas

Looking for more ideas on using literature to teach the trait of voice? We recommend *Books, Lessons, Ideas for Teaching the Six Traits: Writing in the Elementary and Middle Grades,* published by Great Source. Compiled and annotated by Vicki Spandel. For information, please phone 800-289-4490.

An Ear for Voice

For use with pages 35–39 in the Student Traitbook.

We all have favorite books. Chances are, they're the books with the most voice. Voice is the quality in writing that speaks to us and calls us back to the books we love. In this lesson, students begin to explore the trait of voice by listening, tuning in, and asking that important reader's question: does it have voice or not?

Objectives

Students will begin developing an ear for voice simply by noting how appealing a particular text is.

Skills Focus

- Listening to or reading samples of strong or weak voice
- Discussing strong versus weak voice
- Beginning to develop a personal definition of voice

Time Frame

Allow about 20 minutes for this lesson, excluding Setting Up the Lesson and any extensions.

Setting Up the Lesson

If favorite books are the ones with the most voice, favorites might be a great place to begin. Brainstorm a list of your students' favorite books. It may be helpful to have some books on display to help them remember! Add some of your favorites to the list, too—including some that may not be children's books. Remember, these are not necessarily all books you will read to students; just tell why you like them. If you like, read a favorite passage or two. Help students understand that voice is what draws us to many books.

Read the introduction to Unit 3 (Student Traitbook page 35) as students follow along. Ask how many have heard the word *voice* connected to writing before. Ask them to think about what voice is as you begin Lesson 9.

Teaching the Lesson

Read

In this opening part of the lesson, students distinguish voice in three passages, two of which are strong and one of which is very dull and dry! They should have little trouble hearing the difference. Read the passages aloud to yourself prior to the lesson so you can read with expression, if reading aloud. Remind students that they will need to answer an important question

by checking a blank at the end of each passage.

Read Sample 1 aloud or have students read to themselves. Explain that *gruesome* means "frightening and horrible" and *slay* means "kill." Allow time for students to record their responses. Follow the same procedure for Samples 2 and 3.

Share with a Partner

Following each sample, have students compare their responses with those of a partner. Remind them to listen thoughtfully to their partner's ideas, as well as sharing their own. They do not need to agree, but they should have reasons for their choices.

After sharing all three samples, tally responses for the whole class. For each sample, ask how many wanted to hear more? That is a sign of strong voice. How many felt they had heard enough? That's a sign of weak voice. Be sure you talk about reasons for each response. Compare your students' responses with our thoughts:

Sample 1 (Dragon slaying)
Did most find the voice strong? They should. It's light but with a few chills, too!

Sample 2 (Skateboarding)
Did most find the voice strong? We hope not! It is very flat!

Sample 3 (Dog & cat)
Did most find the voice strong? They should. It's lively and humorous.

Write

This is your students' opportunity following this lesson to write down what they think of voice now. Encourage them to think about all the reasons they liked certain books or certain passages you read. Remember, you can keep adding to your thoughts throughout the year.

Scribbles Has a Question

Can colors have voice? Absolutely! What are your students' favorite colors? Make a list. It's the same with foods. Again, make a list. As you consider what to tell Scribbles, students will quickly understand this idea: voice = appeal.

A Writer's Secret

Make sure all students know what an exclamation point looks like. Suggest that exclamation points have the most power if they appear occasionally. Ask students to read Scribbles' three sentences and then choose one that will benefit from an exclamation point. They should not put exclamation points after all three or the power of one will be lost. Each student gets to choose, and they might choose differently. Talk about this.

Extending the Lesson

- Sometimes using a word too many times can kill voice in a piece of writing. Read Sample #2 from the lesson one more time and ask if there is a word used too many times.

(Yes! **Fun**.) Ask students to underline that word each time it is used. Brainstorm some alternatives (you might wish to write the passage on an overhead so everyone can see this.) How many "funs" can you replace?

- Remind students that interesting words make voice stronger. Read either Sample #1 or Sample #3 again and ask students to pick out some of their favorite words.

- Post students' definitions of voice to make a collage. Keep adding as you go through the year and read additional pieces that are strong in voice.

Advanced Extensions

- Pictures can have voice, too. As you read either Sample 1 or Sample 3, invite students to think about the images that come into their minds and to create pictures with voice.

- Invite students to try writing their own pieces about skateboarding (or any sport of their choice). Remind them of two secrets to strong voice: 1. Say what you really think. 2. Use interesting words. Read two or three of the resulting samples aloud and talk about voice.

A Bouquet of Voices

For use with pages 40–43 in the Student Traitbook

Every voice is a little different. We can think of words to describe different kinds of voices, from happy and comical to sad or spooky. Writers can change their voices from time to time. The voice in a recipe might be different from the voice in a story or poem. But changing your own voice is a little like changing your clothes; it's still you inside!

Objectives

In this lesson, students fine-tune their "ear" for voice by thinking of specific words to describe different voices.

Skills Focus

- Listening for voice
- Brainstorming descriptive words to tell what each voice is like
- Discussing the concept of voice with partners and with the class

Time Frame

Allow about 20 minutes for this lesson, excluding Setting Up the Lesson and any extensions.

Setting Up the Lesson

The focus of this lesson is on hearing differences in voices. This can be easily demonstrated with speaking voices. Check to make sure that students know what a bouquet is and how to pronounce it (bō KAY). You need four volunteers from your class and four real or paper cut-out balloons. They will stand at the back of the room so that other students cannot see who is speaking. Ask each student, in turn, to speak the same line. See if the other students can identify the speaker. They will likely find this quite easy. Ask how they knew. (Because each person's voice is unique!) Ask them to describe the person's voice, and write the describing word(s) on the balloon. Give the balloon to the speaker to keep. Remind students that the idea is to make their writing voices as distinctive as their speaking voices. Could your readers identify you just by the sound of your writing? That's voice!

Read the introduction aloud, and let students know that they will be filling in some voice balloons of their own!

Teaching the Lesson

Read

Read the directions aloud as students follow along. Remind students that as they read or listen to each sample, they will need to think of a word or two to describe the sample. If students are going to read on their own, suggest that they read out loud quietly to themselves. Hearing a selection is the best way to identify voice. Students will work with partners to do this.

Ask students to work with their partners to write on as many of the three lines as they can with words that describe the voice in each sample. Remind them that if they cannot think of the right word, they can borrow one from the balloon bouquet at the beginning of the lesson. However, they are always free to come up with a word of their own! When they have finished, share a few of the words they came up with. This is an activity you will want to repeat as you share books aloud through the year. Your students will become increasingly proficient in finding the "right" words to describe what they hear.

Scribbles Has a Question

Read the text as students follow along. Talk about the different "flavors" of voice. Did your students come up with many different words to describe the voices they heard? Does voice come in many flavors? Is this a good thing? (Absolutely.)

A Writer's Secret

Read the first part of the directions aloud as students follow along. You may wish to have one or more student volunteers read from the list of homophones. Ask how many of your young writers have ever used the wrong sound-alike word. Do you do this? Let them know of any homophones that stump you!

Ask students to look at the sample sentence. Do the words all look right? (No.) Ask them to cross out any word that is wrong and to write the correct version right above. Use an editor's caret ∧ to make the insertion. Show students how to do this. Remind them that if you forget a word or need to change a word, sometimes you can use a caret. You do not always need to write the sentence over!

Extending the Lesson

• What do your students' own voices sound like? Ask them to look at a piece of their own writing and to come up with one or more words to describe it. Write your words on balloons (you can draw these and cut them out) and make a bulletin board display.

• Of the three voices you shared in this lesson, which one was the favorite? Talk about why. Start an "awards system" (red dots, silver stars, etc.) to identify books or other writings you and your students feel are especially strong in voice and continue this practice throughout the year. Decide how awards will be given: e.g., two-thirds of the class must agree that the voice is strong. Of course, the samples will need to be read aloud as you vote!

Advanced Extensions

• Choose a sample from this lesson or any other sample to read in full. After hearing the whole piece, what words would you and your students use to describe the voice?

• Invite students to write short notes to any one of the authors whose work you read aloud for this lesson, commenting on their voice. They might say why they like the voice, how they would describe it, ask for advice on writing, or even offer a suggestion for keeping voice strong. Read some notes aloud and post some (or make a class book).

Hear Me Roar!

For use with pages 44–47 in the Student Traitbook

As you and your students discovered in Lesson 10, we all have distinctive speaking voices. Our writing voices are just as distinctive, only most of us haven't used them nearly as much as we've used our speaking voices. This lesson invites the writing voices to come out—and roar!

Objectives

Students will select a personally important or appealing topic and create an original piece of writing to show off their individual voices.

Skills Focus

- Choosing a personally important or interesting topic
- Drawing a picture based on that topic
- Creating an original piece of writing based on that topic and picture
- Sharing and discussing personal writing with a friend
- Finding a word or words to describe one's personal voice

Time Frame

Allow about 20 minutes for this lesson, excluding Setting Up the Lesson and any extensions.

Setting Up the Lesson

Voice tends to be stronger when writers choose their own topics. That's why this lesson is about making choices. You can model this kind of choice by sharing with your students some things you might write about. List three or four possibilities. Don't try to make your topics too dramatic or impressive. After you list your topics (on the overhead or chalkboard), invite students to make their own lists. Each student should try to think of at least three possible things to write about. Give them a few minutes; then share a few of the topics they come up with. Hearing other people's ideas is a great way of adding to your own list.

Teaching the Lesson

Think, Know, Care, Choose!

When students are ready, direct their attention to the list of topics under Some Writing Ideas. They should read through the list to see if they like any of these topics. Then, they should look at the personal lists they brainstormed—they may already have a topic they like better than any of these. The idea is for each writer to choose the topic he/she likes best and has the most to say about. When they have chosen topics, ask them to write their choices in the appropriate blank.

Draw First

Drawing is a wonderful prewriting and writing activity. It prompts thinking and also allows students additional expression of ideas. Students can draw on the page, or pass out appropriate paper of your choice and invite them to create pictures connected with their topics. Encourage use of color and detail.

Write Next

What are the things to keep in mind as students write? Important details and voice. Remind them to look at their pictures often to get additional ideas.

Share

Ask students to "share with themselves" as a first audience. They should read their own writing softly aloud, asking if it makes sense and if it has voice. It is fine to make changes or add any details they forgot. Then, they should share their writing and drawing with a friend. As they listen to each other, they should listen for voice.

Describe Your Voice

Students will describe their own voices—with a partner's help. They should fill in all three balloons if possible—but at least two! It is OK to look back at the words from Lesson 10 for ideas, but many students will not need to do this. Be sure you fill in some balloons for yourself as well and share yours with students!

Share

Share two or three of your students' word balloons with the rest of the class. Talk about how many different kinds of voices there are.

Scribbles Has a Question

How can you tell if your writing has voice? Possible answers: You like it! You read it aloud and listen to the sound. It sounds like the way you talk. You know it says what you really think and feel. You can think of a word (or words) to describe it. You share it with a friend—and the friend likes it.

A Writer's Secret

Make sure everyone knows what an adjective is. Adjectives can also be called describing words. Make sure this term is clear, too. Ask students what happens in their minds when the writer adds the words *snarling* (snarling dog) and *yellow* (yellow teeth). Do they see more? Is it scarier? If it's scarier, is that voice? (Yes.)

Now, ask them to add their own describing words (adjectives) to the sentence about the boy and the horse. Read two or three of the resulting sentences aloud.

Extending the Lesson

- Ask students to look at their own writing one more time. Is there even one word they would like to change? See if this makes a difference in the voice.

- Having personally important topics is key to voice. Show students how to keep a personal list in a notebook, journal, or writing folder. Suggest adding to the list or changing it often so new topics are always appearing. As a group, brainstorm some new possibilities.

Advanced Extensions

- Ask students to write a short (three to five sentences) paragraph about a place they like or do not like. What will they do to put in voice? First, try to picture the place in their minds. Drawing a picture may help. Think of the most interesting details to share. Let their real feelings come through.

- Choose one good sentence from any read-aloud text. Before showing or reading it to students, change one or two of the most interesting words to something flat and voiceless. Then, share the sentence. Ask if there are any words your students would like to change to put more voice into the writing. Brainstorm possible changes. Then, share the author's original text. Talk about the differences between your words and the author's original words.

More Voice, Please!

For use with pages 48–51 in the Student Traitbook

Unfortunately, voice isn't like food. We can't just ask for more. Once writing is committed to paper, we don't usually have the luxury of talking to the writer. But we can feel quite unsatisfied. This lesson offers students additional practice in identifying low-voice pieces, along with some very simple strategies for making voice stronger.

Objectives

Students will recognize low voice in writing read aloud and will know how to apply several strategies to increase voice.

Skills Focus

- Recognizing lack of voice in a piece
- Knowing several strategies for adding voice
- Applying one or more strategies to increase the voice in a given piece
- Sharing and discussing before and after samples with a partner

Time Frame

Allow about 20 minutes for this lesson, excluding Setting Up the Lesson and any extensions.

Setting Up the Lesson

Voice satisfies our ears much the way food satisfies our stomachs. You can illustrate this with a "snack". Tell students you are going to share a snack—then pass out small goodies. Ask how many feel full. Chances are, not many! Would they like more? Sure. Tell them this mini-snack was like a piece of low-voice writing. It leaves you wanting more!

Then, pass out the real snack. The real snack is a high-voice piece. It's more satisfying. Let students know that in this lesson they will be learning ways to make sure their readers get a high-voice "snack" every time.

Teaching the Lesson

Read

Remind them that as you read aloud, they should be asking whether the voice is "satisfying" or leaves them hungry for more. Read Sample 1 aloud, and pause while students respond by putting an X in the appropriate blank. When everyone has finished, read Sample 2 aloud, and again, pause while students respond by putting an X in the appropriate blank.

Think and Share

Talk about which sample, 1 or 2, your students liked better and why. Most should choose Sample 2 as the "satisfying" sample. It has detail, color,

and feelings. Sample 1, by contrast, has no interesting details and no feelings; it's just a report of the facts.

Think and Revise

Pause to be sure everyone understands the activity: to revise a short four-sentence piece for voice. Emphasize that students do not need to rewrite the piece unless they want to. They can make small changes by inserting words or adding a sentence. Remind them how to use the editor's caret: ∧ .

Go slowly through the list of ideas for putting in more voice. Pause if you need to explain any of these ideas. Remind students that they do not need to do all these things! Encourage them to try as many as they can and to check off each one they try.

Share with a Partner

When students have had time to make short, quick changes, give them a minute or two to share with partners. Did people do different things?

Scribbles Has a Question

Ask how many students feel the same way. Do they like to make changes? Or is it hard? Scribbles is wondering if one small change could make a difference. Could it? What do your students think?

A Writer's Secret

Sometimes, being honest in writing can feel uncomfortable. But sharing true feelings is vital to voice. Read the two versions of Juan's writing aloud as your students follow along. In the first, Juan is polite, but he does not really say much. In the second version, Juan shares his true feelings. Does it have more voice? Definitely. Talk about the differences. **NOTE:** The purpose of this reminder is not to encourage students to complain! It is just as important to be honest about good feelings. What matters is to make sure what is on paper matches what you really feel and think.

Extending the Lesson

- Read several (3 or more) short selections aloud from various authors and ask students to rate them as "skimpy snacks" or "filling snacks." Was their hunger for voice satisfied? Talk about why or why not.

- Make a list of all the ways to add voice to writing. The list under Think and Revise will give you a good start. In addition, you might think of any or all of these:

  – Adding describing words

  – Reading aloud and changing what does not sound right

  – Using an exclamation mark

  – Making sure your writing sounds like you

  – Choosing a topic you know about

  – Choosing a topic you care about

Advanced Extensions

- Honesty is a critical element of voice. Consider the rainy day example. Suppose a writer did not like rainy days.

  I know some people like rainy days. I don't! It is boring to be shut up inside. I want to go out, but I don't like getting wet. My clothes get soaked and my hair gets all slicked down. Give me a sunny day!

Read this aloud to students. Ask what they think. Is it good to be honest, even if you sound a little grouchy? (Yes.)

- One writer did the following revision of the rainy day paper. Read it aloud to students or print a copy on an overhead or on the chalkboard. See how many changes they can identify:

  Some people think rainy days are boring. Rainy days are exciting! There are lots of things to do on a rainy day. I go right out and ride my bike through the puddles. Whoosh!

Talk about the voice. Did the changes make the voice stronger? (Yes.)

Voice

Teacher's Guide pages 41, 146–160
Overhead numbers 9–12

Objective

Students will review and apply what they have learned about the trait of voice.

Reviewing Voice

Review with students what they have learned about the trait of voice. Ask students to discuss what voice means and to explain why voice is important in a piece of writing. Then, ask them to recall the main points about voice that are discussed in Unit 3. Students' responses should include the following points:

- Listen for voice.
- Describe voice.
- Pick a topic you know and care about to express your own voice.
- Add voice to flat writing.

Applying Voice

To help students apply what they have learned about the trait of voice, distribute copies of the Student Rubric for Voice on page 41 of this Teacher's Guide. Students will use these to rate one or more of the sample papers that begin on page 114. The papers for voice are also on the overhead transparencies 9–12.

Before students look at the papers, explain that a rubric will help them determine how strong a piece of writing is for a particular trait. Preview the Student Rubric for Voice, pointing out that a paper very strong in voice is rated as "Made it!" and a paper very weak in voice is rated as "It's a start." Tell students to read the rubric and then read the paper they will rate. Then, tell them to look at the paper and the rubric together to determine the rating the paper should receive. Encourage students to make notes on each paper to help them evaluate it. For example, they might put a check mark next to any strong adjectives they use.

Word Choice

Overview

Some writers always seem to find *just* the right words to get the message across or create the images they want. Are they just lucky? Sometimes, probably. It's more likely, though, that they search hard for those "just right" words, much the way a friend searches for the perfect gift. Words *are* a gift to the reader. They help the reader understand the writer's message and feel a part of the writer's world.

The focus of instruction in this unit will be
- Noticing repetition
- Revising to eliminate repetition in writing
- Understanding what a verb is
- Using verbs to give writing life and sparkle
- Using contextual clues to discover meanings of new words
- Using drawing as a way of clarifying word meanings
- Noticing sensory words in writing
- Using sensory words to create vivid, appealing writing

Word Choice: *A Definition*

Word choice depends on choosing the "just right" words to fit audience, topic, and purpose. Secrets to successful word choice include simplicity, use of powerful verbs, sensitivity to nuances of meaning, use of sensory words that put a writer right at the scene, and an expanded vocabulary. For this reason, it is vital that young writers also be readers and listeners, constantly adding to their cache of powerful words and phrases.

The Unit at a Glance

The following lessons in the *Teacher's Guide* and practice exercises in the *Student Traitbook* will help develop understanding of the trait of word choice. The Unit Summary provides an opportunity to practice evaluating papers for word choice.

Unit Introduction: Word Choice

Teacher's Guide pages 56–60	The unique features of the trait of word choice are presented along with a rubric and a list of recommended books for teaching word choice.

Lesson 13: Not Again!

Teacher's Guide pages 61–63 *Student Traitbook pages 52–56*	In this lesson, students listen for repetition and brainstorm some new words or phrases.

Lesson 14: Verb Power!

Teacher's Guide pages 64–66 *Student Traitbook pages 57–60*	In this lesson, students learn what a verb is, compare powerful and flat verbs, and create writing using these important action words.

Lesson 15: Use the Clues

Teacher's Guide pages 67–69 *Student Traitbook pages 61–64*	Given the right reader's strategies, young writers can learn to harvest new words and make them their own.

Lesson 16: Tickling the Senses

Teacher's Guide pages 70–72 *Student Traitbook pages 65–68*	In this lesson, students read, draw, and write to explore the value and fun of sensory language.

Unit Summary: Word Choice

Teacher's Guide pages 73 *Overhead numbers 13–16*	Use the student rubric on page 59 and the activities in the Summary to practice assessing writing for the trait of word choice. At the primary level, we strongly encourage the use of verbal descriptors rather than numbers. The recommended rubrics are designed to support this philosophy. (For those who wish to use numbers for purposes of assigning classroom grades, 5-point and 6-point primary rubrics for teachers, along with a suggested scoring procedure, appear in the Appendix of this Teacher's Guide, pages 201–214.)

Teacher Rubric for Word Choice

Made it!

This is a strong effort. Words convey meaning clearly and help take the reader into the writer's world.

_____ It is easy to picture what the writer is talking about; words paint images in your mind. All words are clear and used correctly.

_____ Repetition is rare. The writer seems to find that "just right" word or phrase to convey each thought.

_____ Strong verbs show action and give life to the piece.

_____ The writer is consistently stretching for new, individual, or fresh ways to express his/her ideas.

_____ Sensory words, as appropriate, add color and life throughout the piece.

Getting there . . .

The paper could use more strong verbs or sensory language, but the good news is, it's on its way! There are many positives.

_____ Much of the time, it is possible to picture what the writer is talking about even if some words are fuzzy or used incorrectly.

_____ A few favorite or familiar words are repeated, but this does not impair meaning.

_____ One or two strong verbs show action, but more would lend additional life.

_____ Once or twice the writer stretches for a fresh or original word or phrase.

_____ Sensory words or phrases, as appropriate, are used at least once.

It's a start.

The writer has made a start by putting something on paper.

_____ It is very difficult to picture what the writer is talking about; the words are not clear or are not used correctly.

_____ Many words are repeated.

_____ Strong verbs are not included in the piece as yet.

_____ The writer is not taking a risk with any new, unusual, or original words or phrases—yet.

_____ Sensory words and phrases might be helpful, but they are not used.

For a rubric with numbers, see the Appendix of this Teacher's Guide, pages 201–214.

Student Rubric for Word Choice

Made it!

___ It is easy to picture what I am saying. I use words correctly.

___ I do not repeat important words.

___ I use strong verbs to show action.

___ I stretch for new words.

___ I use words that help readers see, hear, feel, taste, or smell things.

Getting there . . .

___ Maybe you can picture what I am saying. I think I use most words correctly.

___ I repeat a few words.

___ I use one or two strong verbs to show action.

___ I use one or two new words.

___ I use at least one word to help the reader see, hear, feel, taste, or smell things.

It's a start.

___ It is hard to picture what I am saying. I do not know if I use all the words correctly.

___ I repeat a lot of words.

___ I can't find any strong verbs.

___ I did not try any new words—yet!

___ I did not worry about sights, sounds, smells, tastes, or feelings!

Recommended Selections for Teaching Word Choice

Share a whole book, a chapter, or a favorite passage. As you read aloud, pay particular attention to strong verbs, colorful words, precise phrasing and sensory detail. Ask students questions like these: *Do you have a favorite word or phrase in this passage? Do these words make a picture in your mind? Do any of these words help you see, hear, feel, taste, or smell things? Does the writer repeat any words too often?*

Cannon, Janell. 2000. *Crickwing*. New York: Harcourt, Inc. Young readers will love the misadventures and close calls of Crickwing.

Corey, Shana. 2002. *Milly and the Macy's Parade.* New York: Scholastic, Inc. Based on the historic true story of the young girl who inspired the first Macy's parade.

Hesse, Karen. 1999. *Come On, Rain!* New York: Scholastic. The celebrational dance of a neighborhood springing back to life in the rain.

Jonell, Lynne. 2002. *Brave Mole.* New York: G. P. Putnam's Sons. Inspired by the events of September 11th, this is a story recounted in the form of a fairy tale that young children will find accessible and soothing.

Kemper, Dave, Ruth Nathan, Patrick Sebranek, and Carol Elsholz. *Write Away.* 2001. Wilmington, MA: Great Source. A highly student-friendly handbook that walks students through every step of the writing process.

Lester, Helen. 2002. *Tackylocks.* Boston: Houghton Mifflin. A whimsical and delightful adaptation of *Goldilocks and the Three Bears.*

Micklethwait, Lucy, developer and editor. 1992. *I Spy: An Alphabet in Art.* New York: Green Willow Books. An alphabet book that builds vocabulary even as it sharpens observational skills.

Spandel, Vicki, Ruth Nathan and Laura Robb. *Daybook of Critical Reading and Writing, Grade 2.* 2003. Wilmington, MA: Great Source. The best of modern literature combined with writing tasks that enhance word choice.

Steig, William. 1987. Abel's Island. New York: Farrar, Straus and Giroux. Abel and Amanda set out on a romantic picnic, only to have their day turned into a nightmarish adventure by a wild rainstorm.

Teague, Mark. 2002. *Dear Mrs. LaRue: Letters From Obedience School.* New York: Scholastic. Mrs. LaRue decides to send Ike (the dog) to obedience school, where he learns how to write some pretty terrific letters.

Thompson, Kay. 2002. *Eloise Takes a Bawth.* New York: Simon and Schuster. In this charming encore, Eloise and her beloved Nanny go through the trauma of taking a bath in a luxury hotel—with wild and zany results.

Not Again!

For use with pages 52–56 in the Student Traitbook

Repetition in a song or poem can sometimes provide emphasis and be a plus. However, when a writer just cannot think of another word to use, the result is dull and monotonous. It's also preventable. The writer can strengthen his/her vocabulary by borrowing words from reading or conversation. The writer also must check his or her writing, looking carefully for repetition and taking time to replace tired words with some fresh recruits.

Objectives

Students will learn to notice monotonous repetition in their own text or that of others and will practice making real word "choices" to give writing variety.

Skills Focus

- Noticing repetition in text
- Revising repetitious text by brainstorming alternative word choices
- Creating sentences that do not rely on repetition

Time Frame

Allow about 20 minutes for this lesson, excluding Setting Up the Lesson and any extensions.

Setting Up the Lesson

Before beginning this lesson, read the introduction to Unit 4: Word Choice to students on Student Traitbook page 52. Help students understand that writers must make choices about which words will help the reader understand the writer's message.

Introduce this lesson by helping students understand *repetition*. See how long it takes for your students to notice this as you introduce Lesson 13: *Good morning! In today's lesson, we'll talk about repeating words. Repeating words means saying them over and over. Repeating words can be dull. Repeating words can be monotonous. Repeating is what we will talk about in today's lesson.*

Read the introduction to Lesson 13 (from the Student Traitbook) aloud as students follow along. Ask how many have favorite words they might be repeating too often in their own writing. Let them know that this is a problem for all writers.

Teaching the Lesson

Read
In this opening part of the lesson, students listen or read to notice repeated words in a short passage called "The Scary Dog." Give them a minute to read the directions under Read. Then, read aloud "The Scary Dog" to them or have students read it to themselves.

Think and Share
Ask students to talk about "The Scary Dog" with a friend. What word or idea is repeated too often? (forms of the word *scare*) When students have had time to talk with partners, talk with the whole class: what is the effect on your ears and your mind when the writer uses one kind of word too many times? Brainstorm some alternatives for scary. (*frightening, horrifying, hair-raising, hair curling, menacing, alarming, monstrous, dreadful, fearsome, perilous, grisly*)

Read and Think
Students are asked to read a short passage ("A Really Nice Time") on their own. Remind them to read one time to notice repeated words, then a second time to circle the repeated words. When students have finished circling, ask them to share their thoughts. How many circled the words "really nice"?

Think and Revise
This is your students' opportunity to think of some alternatives to "really nice." Have students work on their own versions of "A Really Nice Time," filling in as many blanks as they can. Be careful! They do not want to repeat their "revisions" either.

Share

Ask students to share their new words with a friend. Do their revisions match? Ask two or three students to share a few of the new words they came up with. Make a class list on the chalkboard or overhead.

Write

Brainstorm together some words that would be easy to repeat too much: *fun, fun time, good, good time, nice time.* Ask students to try avoiding those words as much as possible. Remind students to try to write at least three to five sentences.

Share and Think

Ask students to share their writing with a friend. Remind them what partners do when they share: take turns and listen carefully. They should also fill in the blank to show how they feel about their writing. Talk about how they viewed their own writing.

Scribbles Has a Question

Ask students to share their thoughts on what to tell Scribbles about word choice.

A Writer's Secret

Ask how many of them are remembering to put new words into their personal dictionaries or on their word lists. If you can think of an example, share one word you have added to your own word list lately. Ask for student volunteers to share some words they have added, too.

Extending the Lesson

- Share your own short paragraph on a fun time with a friend. Ask students to tell you if there are any important words you have used too many times. If they discover one (you may wish to include one on purpose), brainstorm some alternatives.

- Emphasize the importance of reading a selection with particularly strong word choice. (See the list of Recommended Books for Teaching Word Choice, p. 60 of the *Teacher Guide* for ideas). Invite students to comment on favorite words and to add one or more words to their personal dictionaries. Be sure all word meanings are clear as you do this.

Advanced Extensions

- Invite students to look at any piece of their own writing outside of this lesson. They should look and listen as they read aloud for repetition. Then, brainstorm alternatives for at least two repeated words.

- What are some reasons writers repeat words? Brainstorm a list. Possibilities: They do not know enough different words. They do not notice they are doing it. They do not read their writing over to hear the repetition. They do not want to bother with changes.

Verb Power!

For use with pages 57–60 in the Student Traitbook

Verbs are action words. They infuse writing with life and energy. This boosts voice, while making word choice more powerful at the same time. When voice and word choice work together, the message reaches its target: the reader. Almost nothing else a writer can do will have such impact on his/her writing as the use of strong verbs.

Objectives

In this lesson, students learn to listen for strong verbs and gain practice in using action words in their own writing.

Skills Focus

- Understanding the meaning of the term verb
- Reading for verbs in text
- Choosing the stronger of two verbs in a selected piece
- Acting out the meaning of several different verbs
- Defining the word verb in their own words
- Creating an original piece of writing using action words

Time Frame

Allow about 20 minutes for this lesson, excluding Setting Up the Lesson and any extensions.

Setting Up the Lesson

How many things did your students do this morning before school? Ask for a list, and write them in verb form: e.g., wake up, yawn, eat, shower, comb [hair], brush [teeth]. When you have finished your list, explain that the words you have listed together are action words—also known as verbs. Some verbs show big or powerful actions. They give your words energy.

Read the introduction to Lesson 14 aloud as your students follow along. Ask which version they like better: *The eagle* **moved** or *The eagle* **soared**. If they liked **soared**, they will love this lesson.

Teaching the Lesson

Read

Make sure everyone has a pencil. Then, ask them to read the sample sentences aloud (quietly) to themselves. Students should circle the verb they like better. Which one has the power? Which one paints a stronger picture?

Share and Check

They should compare their circled verbs with a friend. Did they make the same choices? When they have had time to talk briefly with a partner, discuss verb choices with the whole class. Most should prefer raced, gobbled, and boomed. These words are more vivid and lively.

Write

Time to brainstorm and think about the meaning of the word verb. Ask for thoughts and write down some of their ideas. Now, ask them to come up with individual definitions and to record these in their copies of the Student Traitbook. Share two or three definitions aloud if you wish.

Write with Verbs

When students write about topics that involve a lot of action (sports, gym class), it is easier to include verbs. This is why we chose the topic of "recess." Students can choose another topic, but preferably it should be something that involves action and movement.

Ask students to write a short (three to five sentences) paragraph using some good action verbs. When they have finished writing, ask them to circle their verbs. Share a few favorites. Then, remind each student to put a star by his or her favorite verb.

Scribbles Has a Question

Read the text as students follow along. Then, see how many verbs your students can come up with to identify or describe Scribbles' actions. Make a list if you wish.

A Writer's Secret

Read the text aloud as students follow along. Ask if anyone has had this problem—forgetting a word. Do you do this in your writing?

Ask them to notice the difference between Scribbles' first sentence about the dog and his second. He forgot the word chased. Now, Scribbles has written another sentence: *The cat on the chicken.* Ask students to rewrite the sentence using any verb that fits. Possibilities:

The cat **pounced** on the chicken.
The cat **jumped** on the chicken.
The cat **dropped** on the chicken.

Extending the Lesson

• Read a passage aloud that contains strong verbs. Choose a book you love or pick one from the List of Recommended Books for Teaching Word Choice (p. 60 of this Teacher's Guide). Ask students to listen for favorite verbs as you read. Make a list. Post your list somewhere and keep adding to it through the year. Also, invite students to incorporate some of the words into their personal dictionaries.

• Write notes to parents or to another class using some strong verbs. Good topics for notes: a field trip, gym class, animals.

• Write the verbs from the list below on an overhead transparency or on a chalkboard. Write them in big letters so your students can read them easily. Tell students that they will need to stand up for this activity, but

remind them not to crowd others. Now, point to the words on the verb list one by one, and give students a chance to act out each verb. Ask them if they can feel the strong verbs as they act them out.

wave (at your teacher)

march (in place)

stand (tall and straight)

shake (your body)

nod (your head)

jump (up and down)

Advanced Extensions

• Act out some more verbs. Make some 3 x 5 cards, each with a verb printed clearly on one side. Pass out three or four of these at a time and invite each student to act out his/her verb without showing it to the rest of the class. See if they can guess what it is.

• Watch something that moves: e.g., a bird, a kite, a child. Brainstorm some verbs to describe the movement you see. Invite students to use any verbs you brainstorm to create a free-verse (no rhyming necessary) "Motion Poem" of four to six lines. Each line should include at least one verb.

Lesson
15

Use the Clues

For use with pages 61–64 in the Student Traitbook

Detectives use clues to solve a crime. Criminals, of course, do not usually leave clues on purpose—but good writers do. In fact, good writers are experts at weaving in just the clues a reader needs to figure out the meaning of a passage. This lesson focuses on using those clues well.

Objectives

Students will learn to "use the clues" to figure out or make a best guess about the meaning of a word based on how it is used in context.

Skills Focus

- Reading for new words
- Thinking about how a word is used
- Guessing the meaning of a word from how it is used
- Using art to extend understanding of word meaning

Time Frame

Allow about 20 minutes for this lesson, excluding Setting Up the Lesson and any extensions.

© Great Source. Copying is prohibited.

Setting Up the Lesson

This lesson is about clues. Ask students to imagine this scenario. You have just made a batch of delicious chocolate chip cookies. You go in the other room for a few minutes, and when you return, one of the cookies is missing! How did this happen? Then, you notice the kitchen window is open just a crack—about two inches. Along the outside window sill are tiny paw-prints—about the size of the end of your thumb. There is not one crumb left behind. OK—who's the culprit? (A squirrel or chipmunk most likely—but let students guess for themselves.) How do you know? Clues, of course: small opening, tiny pawprints, no crumbs. Explain that in this lesson, students will be using writing clues to solve the mystery of word meanings. Good writers provide good clues!

Teaching the Lesson

Read for New Words

Read the sentence on page 61 of the Student Traitbook aloud, while students follow along.

Ask students to look at the passage again, and think hard about what the writer is saying. What do they think the word *lashed* means? Why do they think so?

Ask students to share their definitions of the word lashed with a friend. Once they have had time to share with partners, talk about the word with the whole class. Be sure to talk about the clues the writer provides: it's a cat's tail, it is moving in an angry way, etc. Possible meanings: *whipped, twitched, swished, slammed, whacked, thumped.*

Read and Think

Read the passage aloud so that all students get the general meaning. It has five words marked in bold type. Students should reread to focus on figuring out the meanings of these five words, and write their best guesses in the margin where it says "My Notes."

Drawing It Out

Drawing is an excellent prewriting activity—but it can also be useful for clarifying meaning in a writer's or reader's mind. Make sure everyone has drawing tools. Remember—color adds detail!

Remind students that they will draw two pictures. The first picture is meant to help illustrate the concept of effective. The second is to illustrate rundown, abandoned, and littered. Allow time for students to draw in a detailed way. When they have finished, ask them to look again at the notes they made in the margins. Would they change anything?

Ask students to share pictures and definitions. When they have had time to talk with partners, review their definitions, allowing students to speak first. Then, clarify and help them expand their definitions. Ask which of the five words they would like to add to their own personal dictionaries. Provide time for this.

Scribbles Has a Question

Ask students to think and draw first; then, talk about the meaning of Scribbles' name. "Scribble" can mean to write in a hasty or hurried way. Is that a good name for our little friend? Why?

A Writer's Secret

Ask how many students already look for new words. If you have a personal dictionary or journal list, share it so students can have a look. Share some of the words you have added recently.

Extending the Lesson

- Students have already drawn pictures to express the meanings of the five new words from this lesson. Now, invite them to write sentences to go with their pictures, using those five new words.

- Share a sample of well-written text that includes one or more words your students might not know. Prior to reading, write the words on an overhead transparency or on the chalkboard. Then, invite them to listen for those words as you read. Finally, use clues from the text to guess what the meaning of each word might be. Clarify meanings when you finish.

Advanced Extensions

- Provide students with a word that might be new and a sample of text that offers some clues about meaning. Give them a day to look for other clues such as talking to adults or looking in a dictionary. Then, ask them to teach the word to others by drawing a picture and writing one or more sentences that help define the word clearly.

- How do you suppose Ragweed felt exploring? Ask students to write a short note in that character's voice, using one or more of the new words from this lesson.

Tickling the Senses

For use with pages 65–68 in the Student Traitbook

Humans are sense-oriented creatures. We are always aware of sights, sounds, smells, feelings, and tastes—even if it's only subconscious. In this lesson, you'll talk about the importance of putting sensory details into writing to create vivid impressions for the reader.

Objectives

Students will recognize sensory details in the text of others and gain practice in using sensory words in their own writing.

Skills Focus

- Understanding what the five senses are
- Reading for words or phrases that suggest sights, sounds, smells, tastes, or feelings
- Creating a piece of art that suggests connections to as many of the five senses as possible
- Creating an original piece of writing to complement the art

Time Frame

Allow about 20 minutes for this lesson, excluding Setting Up the Lesson and any extensions.

Setting Up the Lesson

Most students write about things they see—and some about things they hear, too. Feelings, smells, and tastes are often left out; yet they add so much to vivid detail. Show students how important other senses can be with this simple activity. Bring a popcorn popper into your classroom. Do not let students know you have it. Ask all students to blindfold themselves or put their hands over their eyes. Start the popper. What do they hear? Ask them to describe it. As the corn begins to pop, what do they smell? Describe it.

Read the introduction to Lesson 16 from the Student Traitbook aloud as your students follow along. Then—pass out some of the popcorn. How does it feel on their tongues? How does it taste? Review the five senses and make sure everyone knows what they are. Remind students that smells, feelings, and tastes can add a lot of detail to any piece of writing.

Teaching the Lesson

Read and Make Notes
Remind them that a good writer doesn't always use the words *smells like, tastes like,* and so on. But certain words make us think of smells and tastes, etc. These are the words they should listen and look for as you or they read the passage from *The Chocolate Touch*

aloud. They need pencils in their hands so they can underline as you go.

Read the passage aloud. Give your students plenty of time for underlining.

Think and Write
Students are asked to fill in a sensory chart. This chart can look big to little writers, so remind them that they should try to think of one thing for each category.

Ask students to share their ideas with a friend. Did they choose the same things? Talk about ideas with the whole class. Things you see are easy. Here are some possibilities for the other senses:

Hear: talking to Mother
Feel: arm around shoulders, kissing her sticky cheek
Smell: chocolate
Taste: not much yet—but the text makes us think of chocolate!

Draw a Place
Tell students that as they choose a place, they should think of one that has interesting details. Patrick Skene Catling wrote about having a chocolate touch because he wanted to include all those good details. Provide tools for drawing.

Write to Tickle
The idea is to create a piece of writing that goes with the picture. They should include sensory details, but not every

sense has to be included; the details should be natural, not forced.

Ask students to take turns sharing their writing and listening well. Ask for two or three volunteers to share their pieces with the class. Listen for sensory details and give the writer some feedback on this.

Scribbles Has a Question

Ask students if they can now name the five senses without any trouble. Most should be able to do this.

A Writer's Secret

Point out how small the change is in the sample sentence. Can just one word make a difference? Yes! That doesn't mean you can't change more—but you do not always have to. Ask students to look again at their pieces of writing. Can they find a place to add one small detail or change just one word?

Extending the Lesson

- Brainstorm some topics that would connect especially well to different senses. For example, imagine falling on an ant hill or visiting a pig farm or going to a music concert. Which senses would be most important then? Encourage students to add these to their "possible topics" lists in their writing journals.

- What sensory details do your students notice right now in your classroom? Brainstorm some lists. Then, write short paragraphs, showing what it's like to be in your classroom. Pretend someone who has never been there will read them.

Advanced Extensions

- Do a "place play," in which students in groups of five (for the five senses) choose one place to describe. Each student will play one of the senses. Give them time to talk about what each sense will notice. Then, they should take turns describing the place from their special point of view. As they share, see if other students can guess where the place is.

- In Lesson 16, students created pictures and paragraphs about places in which sensory detail was important. Activity papers, like place papers, are especially good for sensory detail, too. Ask your students to think of something they have done in which the five senses were important. Possibilities: bathing a pet, swimming underwater, playing in the snow or rain, walking on the sand, falling, cooking something.

Then, ask them to draw and/or write about this experience. Share results by posting them, making a book, or reading some aloud.

Word Choice

Teacher's Guide pages 59, 161–175
Overhead numbers 13–16

Objective

Students will review and apply what they have learned about the trait of word choice.

Reviewing Word Choice

Review with students what they have learned about the trait of word choice. Ask students to discuss what word choice means and to explain why word choice is important in a piece of writing. Then, ask them to recall the main points about word choice that are discussed in Unit 4. Students' responses should include the following points:

- Notice words that repeat.
- Know what a verb is.
- Use clues to figure out new words.
- Use words that help you see, hear, smell, taste, or feel things.

Applying Word Choice

To help students apply what they have learned about the trait of word choice, distribute copies of the Student Rubric for Word Choice on page 59 of this Teacher's Guide. Students will use these to rate one or more of the sample papers that begin on page 114. The papers for word choice are also on the overhead transparencies 13–16.

Before students look at the papers, explain that a rubric will help them determine how strong a piece of writing is for a particular trait. Preview the Student Rubric for Word Choice, pointing out that a paper very strong in word choice is rated as "Made it!" and a paper very weak in word choice is rated as "It's a start." Tell students to read the rubric and then read the paper they will rate. Then, tell them to look at the paper and the rubric together to determine the rating the paper should receive. Encourage students to make notes on each paper to help them evaluate it. For example, they might cross out any words that repeat.

Overview

With very young writers, fluency begins with the understanding of what a sentence is and the ability to write one complete sentence to express an idea. Gradually, young writers move toward multiple-sentence text, which is an important step towards fluency. Nevertheless, even the youngest writers (including those who are not yet writing multiple sentences) can hear fluency in text read aloud, and in this way, they gain an appreciation for and an understanding of this important writing concept.

The focus of instruction in this unit will be
- Listening for fluency as text is read aloud
- Understanding what a sentence is
- Varying sentence beginnings to increase fluency
- Reading aloud with expression
- Combining sentences to make one longer sentence
- Creating personal text to help develop skill in fluency

Sentence Fluency: *A Definition*

Sentence fluency is the rhythm and flow of writing. It is marked by variety in both structure and length and invites expressive, interpretive reading. While fluency is not the same as grammar, the two are connected. Although we are not focusing on dialogue at Grade 2, natural, expressive dialogue is also a component of fluency.

The Unit at a Glance

The following lessons in the *Teacher's Guide* and practice exercises in the *Student Traitbook* will help develop understanding of the trait of sentence fluency. The Unit Summary provides an opportunity to practice evaluating papers for the trait of sentence fluency.

Unit Introduction: Sentence Fluency

Teacher's Guide pages 74–78   The unique features of sentence fluency are presented along with a rubric and a list of recommended books for teaching fluency.

Lesson 17: Keep It Rolling

Teacher's Guide pages 79–81
Student Traitbook pages 69–73   In this lesson, students are encouraged to keep their ideas "rolling" by creating text that is at least three sentences or more in length.

Lesson 18: Making Changes

Teacher's Guide pages 82–84
Student Traitbook pages 74–77   In this lesson, students listen for repetitious beginnings and make simple changes that add interest to writing.

Lesson 19: Come On, Let's Hear It!

Teacher's Guide pages 85–87
Student Traitbook pages 78–81   Students practice both listening and oral reading skills to fine-tune that ear for fluency.

Lesson 20: Math—A Big PLUS for Writing

Teacher's Guide pages 88–90
Student Traitbook pages 82–85   This concluding lesson focuses on using a math strategy—addition—to improve sentence flow.

Unit Summary: Sentence Fluency

Teacher's Guide page 91
Overhead numbers 17–20   Use the student rubric on page 77 and the activities in the Summary to practice assessing writing for the trait of sentence fluency. At the primary level, we strongly encourage the use of verbal descriptors rather than numbers. The recommended rubrics are designed to support this philosophy. (For those who wish to use numbers for purposes of assigning classroom grades, 5-point and 6-point primary rubrics for teachers, along with a suggested scoring procedure, appear in the Appendix of this *Teacher's Guide*, pages 201–214.)

Teacher Rubric for Sentence Fluency

Made it!

This is a strong effort. The writing flows well from sentence to sentence and is easy to read aloud. It achieves its purpose.

_____ This piece is very easy to read aloud; it has a rhythmic, natural flow.

_____ Many sentences begin in different ways.

_____ Long and short sentences blend, giving the text variety, texture, and interest.

_____ The piece is four or more sentences long, allowing fluency to build.

_____ The writer uses complete sentences (with the exception of a fragment used for effect or emphasis).

Getting there . . .

The paper may have a bumpy moment or two, but the good news is, it's on its way! There are many positives.

_____ The piece is not difficult to read aloud, especially with a little practice.

_____ A few sentences begin in different ways; some beginnings are repeated.

_____ Some sentences are longer than others.

_____ The text runs about three to four sentences in length, so fluency is just gaining some momentum.

_____ The writer uses complete sentences in most cases.

It's a start.

The writer has made a start by putting something on paper.

_____ The piece is difficult to read aloud. The reader needs to practice or reread to get the flow.

_____ Virtually all sentences begin the same way.

_____ Sentences all tend to be about the same length.

OR

_____ The writer may have composed just one or two sentences—so far! This is a beginning, even if the piece does not have a real sense of fluency <u>yet</u>.

_____ The writer may run sentences together or may not write in complete sentences.

For a rubric with numbers, see the Appendix of this Teacher's Guide, pages 201–214.

Student Rubric for Sentence Fluency

Made it!

___ This is easy to read out loud.

___ A lot of my sentences begin in different ways.

___ I used some short sentences and some long sentences.

___ My paper has four or more sentences.

___ My sentences are complete.

Getting there . . .

___ It is not too hard to read out loud.

___ I used one or two different sentence beginnings.

___ Some sentences are longer than others.

___ My paper is about three or four sentences long.

___ Most of my sentences are complete.

It's a start.

___ It might be hard to read out loud.

___ My sentences all begin with the same words.

___ My sentences are all about the same length.

___ I only wrote one or two sentences—so far!

___ I am not sure if my sentences are complete.

Recommended Books for Teaching Sentence Fluency

Share a whole book or a favorite passage. Ask students questions like these: *Is it easy to listen to? Do you hear variety in sentence length? What about beginnings or sentence patterns? Could you read it with lots of expression?*

Allard, Harry. 1972. *Miss Nelson Is Missing.* Boston: Houghton Mifflin. Sweet Miss Nelson wants her class to behave but cannot without the help of the nightmare substitute teacher, Viola Swamp.

dePaola, Tomie. 2002. *Adelita: A Mexican Cinderella Story.* New York: G. P. Putnam's Sons. A twist on the classic story, told with humor and grace.

dePaola, Tomie. 1996. *The Legend of the Indian Paintbrush.* New York: Putnam and Grosset Group. A lyrical and reverent story based on a Native American legend.

George, Christine O'Connell. 2002. *Little Dog and Duncan.* Boston: Houghton Mifflin. George has a gift for making poetry out of everyday moments.

Grimes, Nikki. 2001. *A Pocketful of Poems.* Boston: Houghton Mifflin. A delightful collection, ringing with the individual voice of poet Nikki Grimes.

Hogrogian, Nonny. 2002. *One Fine Day.* New York: Simon and Schuster. The beloved Armenian folk tale of a fox who steals milk.

Kiesler, Kate. 2002. *Wings on the Wind.* Boston: Houghton Mifflin. A beautifully assembled anthology of 23 poems all about birds.

Marshall, James. 1972. *George and Martha.* Boston: Houghton Mifflin. The delightful and comical escapades of two great friends, everyone's favorite hippos.

Kemper, Dave, Ruth Nathan, Patrick Sebranek, and Carol Elsholz. *Write Away.* 2001. Wilmington, MA: Great Source. A highly student-friendly handbook that walks students through every step of the writing process.

Price, Kathy. 2002. *The Bourbon Street Musicians.* Boston: Houghton Mifflin. A new and rollicking rendition of an age-old folktale.

Spandel, Vicki, Ruth Nathan and Laura Robb. *Daybook of Critical Reading and Writing, Grade 2.* 2003. Wilmington, MA: Great Source. Outstanding excerpts from the best of modern literature featuring numerous read-aloud passages.

Young, Ed. 1989. *Lon Po Po.* New York: Penguin Putnam. Red Riding Hood story from China features three clever children who manage to outwit the wolf.

Keep It Rolling

For use with pages 69–73 in the Student Traitbook

Have you ever heard just the first two or three notes of a song on the radio only to have someone turn it off? Frustrating, isn't it? You never really got the feel or flow of it. Written text is like that; you need to see or hear enough to get a sense of its rhythm and flow, too. In this lesson, students are encouraged to write more than a sentence or two so the fluency can come through and keep the ball rolling.

Objectives

Students will use observational skills to discover how extended text lets fluency build and will try their own hands at creating an original piece of text that is at least three sentences long.

Skills Focus

- Noticing detail in extended text
- Identifying specific features of extended text (e.g., more feeling, sharper word pictures)
- Selecting a topic for personal writing
- Creating a sample of personal writing that is 3 sentences or more long

Time Frame

Allow about 20 minutes for this lesson, excluding Setting Up the Lesson and any extensions.

Setting Up the Lesson

A CD player and a little music are all you need to introduce this lesson. Try playing the first one or two notes to several songs your students might know. Ask them to guess what the songs are. Ask them to hum along! (They can't, of course—unless their guesses are very good or very lucky!) Talk about how you need to hear more than just a note or two to get the sound and rhythm of a song. Explain that writing is like this, too. Sometimes, a reader can feel frustrated with only one sentence. It's good to have two or more sentences to get a real feeling for the writer's rhythm and fluency. Now, play a whole song, and encourage students to join in by singing, humming, or clapping hands.

Read the introduction to Unit 5 (page 69 of the Student Traitbook) to reinforce the idea of fluency. Then, look at the introduction to Lesson 17 with students so that they will understand what part of fluency they will work on first.

Teaching the Lesson

Read

In this opening part of the lesson, students notice the additional detail and voice (feelings) in extended text. Why is it more interesting? Because there is room and time for the writer to give more information and paint more vivid pictures.

Share Sample 1 and Sample 2 out loud or have students read them to themselves. Remind students to notice any differences in the two samples.

Think and Share

Ask students to talk about which of the two samples they liked better. Now, ask them to look at items in the numbered list. Invite students to put an X in the blank before any item they feel is true of Sample 2.

If your students think of any differences not mentioned on the list, ask them to write those in the space provided, and talk about them.

Choose

Ask students to choose an idea they think they could write at least three sentences about. They can come up with an idea of their own (encourage this) or choose one from the list.

Think, Write, and Roll

Students should keep ideas flowing as long as they have something to say without launching into a new topic. The idea is to write at least three sentences.

Ask students to share their paragraphs, taking turns and listening carefully to the sound and the details. Ask how many were able to keep the ball rolling for at least three sentences? Reinforce this by telling them this is the first important step toward fluent writing!

Scribbles Has a Question

Ask students to write Scribbles a short note. Read two or three of these aloud. What do your students think about just stopping after a single sentence?

A Writer's Secret

Go through the checklist together, asking students to mark each item they think is true (all are true).

Extending the Lesson

- Share a one-sentence piece on the chalkboard or overhead. Invite students to ask you questions you can use to extend the piece.

- Next time you start a book, read one sentence and then pretend to stop. See if your students protest. Then, finish the story. Talk about different things writers do to extend the text: tell more about the idea, talk about feelings, create images.

Advanced Extensions

- Many writers find it is easier to keep that writing ball rolling with a letter than with any other kind of writing. Try this with your students. Write letters—to each other, to parents, to people in the business community, or to authors. Ask students to guess how long their letters might be (in sentences). We are betting most will not have trouble writing four sentences or more. Mail the letters, if possible, and make a collection of letters and responses.

- One thing that encourages fluency is choosing a topic about which you have a lot to say. Spend some time brainstorming topics to add to your lists (such as the ones you started in your writer's notebooks or journals). Make a class list and keep it posted for a few days so students can borrow. During that time, provide some extra credit to students who choose one of those topics and write four or more sentences about it.

- Practice recognizing fragments and turning them into sentences. You can begin with a list of five "sentences," two of which are fragments. Ask students to tell you which are which and then to turn the fragments into sentences. Talk about how fragments can sometimes add punch—if they are used on purpose and not too often.

Making Changes

For use with pages 74–77 in the Student Traitbook

Varied sentence beginnings not only keep readers awake, but also often show how ideas connect. Though young writers often begin their multiple-sentence writing by following patterns *(My friend is tall. My friend is nice.)*, we want them to break free of this eventually and begin building some variety into their text. Even one small change can make a huge difference in fluency! This lesson provides young writers a chance to sharpen their ears and their pencils—and make some changes happen!

Objectives

In this lesson, students learn to listen for variety in text and to make changes—small to extensive—that increase variety.

Skills Focus

- Noticing repetition
- Marking text to show repeated patterns
- Revising a short sample of text to start one sentence in a different way
- Creating an original piece of writing in which each sentence begins differently

Time Frame

Allow about 20 minutes for this lesson, excluding Setting Up the Lesson and any extensions.

Setting Up the Lesson

People often write in patterns, but very few of us speak this way! You can show this to students easily by the way you introduce Lesson 18: e.g., *Today we will talk about sentence variety. Today we will read some sentences together. Today we will listen to how the sentences begin.*

Ask students what they notice about the way you are speaking. Ask if it would be more interesting and easier to listen to if you just spoke normally and started some sentences in different ways. Remind them that variety adds interest to writing, too (and it also sounds more natural).

Teaching the Lesson

Read

Ask students to follow along as you read the sample called "At My School" aloud or have students read aloud quietly to themselves. Ask students to rate the passage by putting an X in front of the statement that best describes their reaction. Most students will agree with the second assessment.

Ask for your students' advice. The author started every single sentence the same way. Does he/she need to change them all? Would changing just one be enough? (We think having two that start the same way is plenty! At the same time, remember that your revisers are beginning writers, so making even one change is an important step!)

Revise

The directions in this section are a little complicated. You need to read them aloud as your students follow along. Start with the first part, and talk about differences in the Before and After samples. Do the sentences have the same meaning? Yes. Do they use the same words? Some of the same words— but not all. What is the main difference? The After sentence—the revised sentence—starts with different words.

Now, see if students can do this, working with just one sentence. Be sure there are students working on each sentence. Make sure students underline the sentence they have chosen so they can find it easily and do not get confused. Then, give them time to write their revisions. Write a revision of your own on an overhead transparency so you can show it to students when they are finished.

Ask students to share some of their revisions with a partner before sharing with the class. Talk about the kinds of changes people made.

Write

Ask students to write a short (three to five sentences) paragraph in which every sentence begins differently. They will need to pay attention to their sentence beginnings to make this work. This will be a challenge for some.

Think

Ask students to underline the first three words in each sentence of their paragraph. Are they all the same? If so, see if there is one that can be changed.

Scribbles Has a Question

Talk first about Scribbles' problem. The question is a good opportunity to talk about "gentle sharing," starting with the pronoun "I". Comments that begin with "You" or "Your paper" sometimes sound like accusations. Instead, when a listener says, "**I** heard _____," it helps the writer notice things—without hurt feelings.

A Writer's Secret

Ask how many of them read their own writing aloud to themselves and really listen to the sentence flow. If possible, model this for students during the next few days, reading a piece of your own writing aloud to yourself as they listen in. Think aloud about what you hear, too!

Extending the Lesson

- Read a passage aloud that is strong in fluency. Ask students to listen for differences in sentence beginnings. Repeat this activity with other texts.

- Make copies of a fluent passage to pass out. Ask them to underline the first three words of each sentence and to talk with partners about how many different sentence beginnings they notice. Repeat this activity with other texts.

Advanced Extensions

- Write a simple sentence on the chalkboard or on an overhead transparency. Ask students to rewrite that one sentence as many different ways as they can. Notice that in changing sentence patterns, writers add words, change words, write from a different point of view, or add details. As you do this activity, talk about the many ways you can change sentences.

- Put students in groups of three to do a write-around with sentences. Each person writes one sentence at the top of a sheet of paper. Then, everyone passes to the left. The next person must write another sentence on the same topic—only it must begin with different words. Then, pass again. Each group should now have three sentences, all with different beginnings. Keep going until you cannot think of one more sentence. (NOTE: Two full times around is very good!) Read one or two of the final papers aloud just to make sure all the beginnings are different.

Come On, Let's Hear It!

For use with pages 78–81 in the Student Traitbook

Reading aloud is a good way to check for fluency. When text is fluent, the reading is smooth and easy. Nonfluent text, by contrast, tends to be jarring. The reader may need to pause, go back, or even start over altogether. Sometimes, it's hard to tell where sentences begin or end. In this lesson, students will practice their listening skills, then read aloud with expression—to bring out the fluency of the text.

Objectives

Students will sharpen their skills in listening for fluency as text is read aloud and will use their own oral reading skills to bring out the fluency in written text.

Skills Focus

- Listening for fluency as text is read aloud
- Reading aloud to bring out fluency
- Reading in a group
- Creating a short poem that can be read aloud

Time Frame

Allow about 20 minutes for this lesson, excluding Setting Up the Lesson and any extensions.

Setting Up the Lesson

You can hear fluency when text is read aloud. Even students who do not yet write with fluency themselves can hear fluency in the text of others. Ask students to listen for fluency in this passage:

Fluent writing flows. Fluent writing sounds good. Fluent writing is interesting. Is this fluent writing?

Students will (we hope) say no! Tell them that they will practice listening for fluency in some other passages in this lesson. By the end of the lesson, they will try writing some fluent text.

Teaching the Lesson

Read

Students will listen for fluency in a short passage from the book *Muncha! Muncha! Muncha!* by Candace Fleming. Before sharing the actual text (which is very fluent), test your students' ears for fluency by reading or having students read the adaptation of the Fleming passage, which is Sample 1.

When you finish, ask students what they think. Did this piece sound fluent? Or did it seem to stall? Then read or have students read Sample 2, listening again for fluency.

Think

Ask students if this version by the author sounds different from the choppy version you read earlier. Yes! Why? They may mention that the sentences are not short and choppy, and each sentence has more than one small idea. Sentences begin in different ways. This writing sounds smoother—more like the way people really speak.

Also, ask if they think they can read out loud with expression: How many think so? Tell them they all can. It is just a matter of practice. Expression brings out the fluency and the feelings in writing.

Read

Poetry is a natural for fluency because the lines of a poem are usually arranged so that each is a fluent phrase. Before reading the poem itself or the numbered list, break students into groups of four. (If you have groups of three, one student in the group can read an extra line or you can join the group to be the fourth reader.)

Now, make sure everyone can find the Mother Goose poem called "Little Drops of Water." Read it aloud as your students follow along. In each group, students need to number off so each student has one line.

Make sure students feel comfortable with all the words. Read the poem aloud again if you need to. Now, ask students to read their individual lines quietly to themselves. Now, it is time for groups to practice. Spread out in the room so voices are not distracting.

Ask students to arrange themselves in their groups in order. Then, they should read their poems through, line by line, taking turns. Allow a minute or two for this. Now, ask them to practice one more time, only this time, putting lots of expression into their voices.

Write

To help get students started, have them suggest ideas. Make a list on the board for them to use as a reference. Although the poem in the Student Traitbook rhymes, not all poems do. The idea of poetry is to express an idea in relatively few words.

Scribbles Has a Question

Talk about the issue of shyness. Could this keep a person from wanting to read aloud? What would the person miss? Is it OK to be shy? Of course! Many readers and teachers are shy. You can read aloud to yourself first—then maybe to just one friend. Read in a whisper and then in a bigger voice.

A Writer's Secret

Ask if anyone has a solution to this problem of many short sentences. One is to add more detail to one or more of the sentences. Another is to combine two or more sentences into one. (This is actually a preview of the lesson coming up.) If your students do not think of any solutions, ask them to keep thinking about it—and you can always return to this example after Lesson 20 when they should have more ideas.

Extending the Lesson

- Find additional short poems or passages your students can read aloud in small groups. Keep practicing. Encourage expression. Even encourage students to "act out" the parts if they feel comfortable.

- Try some read-aloud practice with dialogue. Dialogue is excellent for bringing out expression. See *George and Martha* by James Marshall (from the list of Recommended Books for Teaching Sentence Fluency, p. 78 of this *Teacher's Guide*) for some short, highly expressive examples.

Advanced Extensions

- Encourage students who feel comfortable doing so to practice reading their own text aloud and then to share with the class. Talk about how reading with expression can help bring out fluency.

- Continue to share samples of fluent writing aloud with your class. Ask them to listen for fluency and to rate them using the Student Rubric for Fluency. Talk about reasons for fluency such as having enough text, varying the sentence beginnings, and writing in an expressive way that's fun to read aloud. Give a Fluency Award to the top contenders. Let students design this award themselves.

Math— a Big PLUS for Writing

For use with pages 82–85 in the Student Traitbook

Though math and writing are different subjects, lessons from one can sometimes help us with the other. For example, take addition. In math, you can add two small numbers to get a bigger number. In writing, you can "add" two small sentences and get a bigger sentence that's often more graceful. It's called sentence combining, and it works magic on fluency—as your students will see.

Objectives

Students will recognize choppy sentences in writing and practice sentence combining as one strategy for eliminating this problem.

Skills Focus

- Recognizing choppiness in writing
- Recognizing short sentences that could be combined
- Combining two, three, or four short sentences into one longer sentence

Time Frame

Allow about 20 minutes for this lesson, excluding Setting Up the Lesson and any extensions.

Setting Up the Lesson

To set up this lesson, you need 50 pennies and some other change. Put the change in piles on a table or desk in front of you where students can see it clearly. Now, ask students to imagine you are at the store buying something that costs 40 cents. What is the best way to pay for it, using the money you have? There are several possible answers to this but see what your students come up with: two quarters (with some change back), a quarter plus a dime plus a nickel, four dimes, etc. Demonstrate several possible ways to make 40 cents out of your money collection. Then, tell them you've decided to pay with pennies only. Count out 40 pennies. Ask what they think of this way of paying. Explain that this is one reason we have bigger currency, such as dollar bills, to make the exchange of money faster and easier.

Now, explain that writing can be like this, too. If we write only in tiny little sentences, it can take a very long time to come to the point. Sometimes, though, we can put two or more little thoughts together in one sentence. Read the introduction to Lesson 20 aloud as students listen.

Teaching the Lesson

Read
Have students listen carefully as you share the three sample sentences about "My dad." When you have finished reading, they should mark their response by putting an **X** in the appropriate blank.

Ask them to look at the example showing how the three sentences could be combined. Does the final sentence have all the smaller ideas in it? Yes.

Read, Think, and Write
Ask students to read the two sentences about Sparkle. When they have finished writing, ask for two or three students to share their single sentences. Share one of your own on the chalkboard or overhead.

Think and Write Again
Read the sample sentences aloud as students follow along. Again, pause while students try combining. Share one or two of their examples and also share your own. Remember that their combinations do not need to match yours. It is important to remind students of this, so they do not get the impression that there is one "right" way to do it.

1 + 1 + 1 + 1 = ONE BIG SENTENCE!
Let students know that this time, they will be putting four sentences together, not just two. It may take more than one

try, and that is fine. It is also fine to "borrow" ideas from the two smaller sentences they have just done. Make sure you do an example too to show them how these four tiny ideas can be combined into one sentence. For example:

My sister's fish Sparkle is blue with black fins.

NOTE: Combining four sentences into one is an advanced task, so do not expect all students to do this.

Pick and Practice
They are asked to combine three small sentences into one larger one. They should choose one: Practice #1 or Practice #2. It is not necessary to do both (but if you have students who are speedy, then encourage them to try both).

Scribbles Has a Question
Can students help Scribbles combine his sentences? You try it, too, and read some results aloud.

A Writer's Secret
Talk about how readers sometimes get excited when they read, and the expression shows in their faces or in their gestures. It means they are engaged with the reading. Do you use gestures when you read? Ask your students! Does your face change expression? Ask!

Extending the Lesson

- Ask students to look at a piece of their writing. Do they see two or three sentences that could be combined? Ask them to do this and then to read the results aloud.

- Continue providing practice in combining sentences. Ask them to try writing the combination sentence in more than one way.

(Don't forget to return to Lesson 19, A Writer's Secret, if that example of short sentences gave your students trouble. They might be able to solve the problem now!)

Advanced Extensions

- The Writer's Secret talks about readers using facial expressions or gestures to reinforce feelings as they read. This is what actors do on television or on the stage. Invite students to watch an actor (in a film, on TV, in a play) and to do a sketch showing an actor using facial expressions or gestures to help bring out fluency as he or she speaks.

- Invite students to do a "flat" reading and an "expressive" reading of the same piece. (Samples should be about 3 to 6 sentences long.) Ask classmates to identify which reading is more expressive and to talk about differences they heard.

Sentence Fluency

Teacher's Guide pages 77, 176–188
Overhead numbers 17–20

Objective

Students will review and apply what they have learned about the trait of sentence fluency.

Reviewing Sentence Fluency

Review with students what they have learned about the trait of sentence fluency. Ask students to discuss what sentence fluency means and to explain why sentence fluency is important in a piece of writing. Then, ask them to recall the main points about sentence fluency that are discussed in Unit 5. Students' responses should include the following points:

- Write enough to let ideas flow.
- Listen for fluency.
- Change sentence beginnings.
- Combine shorter sentences into one longer sentence.

Applying Sentence Fluency

To help students apply what they have learned about the trait of sentence fluency, distribute copies of the Student Rubric for Sentence Fluency on page 77 of this Teacher's Guide. Students will use these to rate one or more of the sample papers that begin on page 114. The papers for sentence fluency are also on the overhead transparencies 17–20.

Before students look at the papers, explain that a rubric will help them determine how strong a piece of writing is for a particular trait. Preview the Student Rubric for Sentence Fluency, pointing out that a paper very strong in sentence fluency is rated as "Made it!" and a paper very weak in sentence fluency is rated as "It's a start." Tell students to read the rubric and then read the paper they will rate. Then, tell them to look at the paper and the rubric together to determine the rating the paper should receive. Encourage students to make notes on each paper to help them evaluate it. For example, they might underline sentence beginnings that are mostly the same.

Overview

Conventions are all about correctness—the "rules of the game." When you teach conventions, you are teaching textual readability, a way of making it easier for the reader to understand the writer's ideas. It is unreasonable to expect flawless text from second grade writers—to whom many conventions are brand new. However, the more errors your student editors can spot and correct on their own, the better.

The focus of the instruction in this unit will be
- Punctuating statements and questions correctly
- Editing to insert spaces between words run together
- Understanding when to use capital letters
- Editing to correct faulty spelling of eight common sight words
- Recognizing and applying two editor's symbols

Conventions: *A Definition*

The trait of **conventions** includes the textual conventions a copy editor would deal with such as spelling, punctuation, usage and grammar, capitalization, and indentation. Visual conventions can also include presentation on the page. While we will not deal with this, it is entirely appropriate to remind students of these considerations when working on a project for which layout is critical.

The Unit at a Glance

The following lessons in the *Teacher's Guide* and practice exercises in the *Student Traitbook* will help develop an understanding of the trait of conventions. The Unit Summary provides an opportunity to practice evaluating papers for the trait of conventions.

Unit Introduction: Conventions

Teacher's Guide pages 92–96   Students are introduced to the unique features of the trait of conventions.

Lesson 21: Telling or Asking?

Teacher's Guide pages 97–99
Student Traitbook pages 86–90

Students listen for the difference between a statement and a question and add punctuation.

Lesson 22: Tools of the Trade

Teacher's Guide pages 100–102
Student Traitbook pages 91–94

Students are introduced to the way editors mark text for correction, learning to apply the correct symbol for "Put a space here."

Lesson 23: Capitals at the Start

Teacher's Guide pages 103–105
Student Traitbook pages 95–98

Students use an editing symbol to correct capitalization errors.

Lesson 24: I Know It on Sight!

Teacher's Guide pages 106–109
Student Traitbook pages 99–102

This lesson offers students practice in spotting and correcting sight words.

Unit Summary: Conventions

Teacher's Guide page 110
Overhead numbers 21–24

Use the student rubric on page 95 and the activities in the Summary to practice assessing writing for the trait of conventions. At the primary level, we strongly encourage the use of verbal descriptors rather than numbers. The recommended rubrics are designed to support this philosophy. (For those who wish to use numbers for purposes of assigning classroom grades, 5-point and 6-point primary rubrics for teachers, along with a suggested scoring procedure, appear in the Appendix of this *Teacher's Guide*, pages 201–214.)

Teacher Rubric for Conventions

Made it! (Check 5 or more)

This is a strong effort. The writing communicates, writer to reader.

_____ Conventions come easily to this writer or he/she has gone over the paper carefully.

_____ The writer put spaces between words.

_____ The spelling is correct or easy to read.

_____ Periods are consistently used to end sentences.

_____ Question marks are consistently used to end questions.

_____ Capital letters are consistently used to start sentences.

Getting there . . . (Check 5 or more)

The paper could clearly use some editing, but it's on its way!

_____ Conventions are clear or correct enough to make the paper readable.

_____ The writer put spaces between most words.

_____ Most of the spelling is readable with attention.

_____ Periods are used to end most (or some) sentences.

_____ Question marks are used to end most (or some) questions.

_____ Capital letters are used to start most (or some) sentences.

It's a start. (Check 4 or more)

The writer has made a start by putting something on paper.

_____ Conventions are very difficult for this writer or he/she has not looked over the paper yet to make grade-level appropriate corrections.

_____ The writer often forgot to put spaces between words.

_____ A lot of the spelling is hard to read.

_____ Periods do not appear at the ends of all sentences.

_____ Question marks do not always end questions.

_____ Capital letters do not always begin sentences.

For a rubric with numbers, see the Appendix of this Teacher's Guide, pages 201–214.

Student Rubric for Conventions

Made it!

___ I read my paper over well.

___ I put spaces between my words.

___ My spelling is easy to read.

___ I used periods to end sentences.

___ I used question marks to end questions.

___ I used capital letters to start sentences.

Getting there . . .

___ I looked at my paper for a minute!

___ I put spaces between most words.

___ Most of my spelling is easy to read.

___ I remembered to use periods some of the time.

___ I remembered question marks some of the time.

___ I used capital letters to start some sentences.

It's a start.

___ I did not read my paper over—yet!

___ I forgot spaces between my words.

___ My spelling is hard to read.

___ I forgot some periods.

___ I forgot to use question marks.

___ I forgot a lot of capital letters.

Recommended Selections for Teaching Conventions

Though we do recommend the use of the handbook *Write Away* (see annotation below), no extended book list is included with this set of lessons because virtually any book can be used to help teach conventions. Point out professional writers' use of periods, question marks or other punctuation; point out use of capital letters, as well. As you share published text, be sure to notice

- various conventions authors have used to make meaning clear.

- authors' use of conventions to enhance voice.

- any conventions that may be new to students.

- any conventions students would change on the basis of personal style.

- any unintentional errors (there are not many in published books, but they do appear.

You will also find numerous lessons to help students work successfully with conventions in the following Great Source handbook:

Kemper, Dave, Ruth Nathan, Patrick Sebranek, and Carol Elsholz. *Write Away*. 2001. Wilmington, MA: Great Source. A highly student-friendly handbook that walks students through every step of the writing process.

For samples of conventions used well, consider this text:

Spandel, Vicki, Ruth Nathan and Laura Robb. *Daybook of Critical Reading and Writing, Grade 2*. 2003. Wilmington, MA: Great Source. Outstanding excerpts from the best of modern literature (nonfiction to poetry).

More Ideas

Looking for more ideas on using literature to teach the trait of conventions? We recommend *Books, Lessons, Ideas for Teaching the Six Traits: Writing in the Elementary and Middle Grades*, published by Great Source. Compiled and annotated by Vicki Spandel. This book contains a teacher resource section that includes references you may find helpful as a writer and teacher of writing. For information, please phone 800-289-4490.

Telling
or Asking?

For use with pages 86–90 in the *Student Traitbook.*

Written text is filled with clues that help the reader figure out the meaning and inflection. For example, periods or question marks show whether a sentence is a question or a statement. Some of these clues can be heard when readers share text aloud, which helps many students fine-tune their punctuation skills.

Objectives

Students will use listening skills to distinguish between statements and questions and will practice applying the appropriate punctuation.

Skills Focus

- Listening to distinguish between statements and questions
- Inserting the appropriate punctuation marks
- Practicing punctuation skills in a short paragraph
- Creating personal writing that uses appropriate end punctuation

Time Frame

Allow about 20 minutes for this lesson, excluding Setting Up the Lesson and any extensions.

Setting Up the Lesson

Before beginning the lesson, introduce students to the trait of conventions by reading and talking about the unit introduction on page 86 of the Student Traitbook. Ask students if they have ever noticed how a speaker's voice changes depending on whether the speaker is telling the listener something or asking a question. To illustrate this, try two sentences about the weather, and ask if they can tell which one is the question just by the shift in your voice:

1. *It's really cold today.*

2. *Is it really cold today?*

Of course, word order provides a clue, too. Ask them to try this with a partner. Each person should ask a question. See if the partner can hear the speaker's voice rise. Then, reverse roles. How many can hear the voices go up a bit at the end of a question? Most, we hope!

Read the introduction to Lesson 21 together—and get ready to listen for statements and questions.

Teaching the Lesson

Question or Statement?
Ask students to share the sentences aloud, one by one, pausing to let students circle the right word for each one.

Think
Ask students to insert the correct marks of punctuation for each sentence. Remind them to read the sentences aloud if they're not sure which mark of punctuation to use. Answers:

1. *statement*

2. *question*

3. *question*

4. *statement*

5. *question*

Ask students to discuss their responses to each sentence. If students' responses do not agree with our suggestions, read the sentence aloud to help them hear the correct punctuation. Remind students to read aloud any time they are checking punctuation in their own work.

Read & Respond
Ask students to read the short piece on their own, inserting the correct punctuation as they go. Remind them to read aloud any time they are unsure.

Ask students to share their paragraphs, comparing punctuation marks. Then, read the paragraph aloud, emphasizing the inflection so they can really hear the punctuation at the end of each sentence:

I took my new remote control car over to my friend's house. He has a brother Jon who is four and a brother Kyle who is two. Can you guess what happened?

Yes, they all wanted a turn with my car.
Who do you think wanted to go first? If
you guessed Jon, you are correct. He
wanted to drive it all day.

Write

Ask students to write a short (three
to five sentences) paragraph about
sharing. (Students can choose a
different topic if they wish.) One of
their sentences should be a question.
Ask students to read their writing
aloud with partners, taking turns.
Partners should listen for statements
and questions and help each other
review the end punctuation.

Scribbles Has a Question

Ask students to discuss the question
of hearing the punctuation in your
head when you read to yourself. Most
students will probably say that they
can "hear" questions even when not
reading aloud. What if they can't?
Practicing aloud can help!

A Writer's Secret

Remind students to check sentence
beginnings and endings every time
they edit. This will ensure that they
find a capital to start the sentence
and punctuation to end it.

Extending the Lesson

• Share a one-sentence piece on the
chalkboard or overhead, but do not
punctuate it. Invite students to tell

you what mark of punctuation
should go at the end. Extend this
exercise with additional practice
sentences or a whole paragraph.

• Read just one paragraph aloud from
a favorite book. First, read the whole
paragraph to get the continuity.
Then, read aloud a second time, this
time pausing after each sentence so
students can write down a period,
question mark, or exclamation point.
Review what they have written when
you finish, and compare it to the
author's original.

Advanced Extensions

• Ask students to review a sample of
their own writing that is at least three
sentences long. Ask them to follow
the "Writer's Secret" from this lesson,
looking over sentence beginnings and
endings. Encourage them to make any
needed changes.

• For fun, create a short practice
paragraph (three to five sentences)
in which every sentence ends with
the wrong mark of punctuation. Be
sure to double space, allowing room
for corrections. Ask student editors
to read for meaning, then to cross out
the wrong mark and insert the right
one just above. Compare results, and
review the correct marks on the
overhead or chalkboard.

Tools of the Trade

For use with pages 91–94 in the *Student Traitbook*.

This lesson is about using spacing to set words apart so that reading is easier.

Objectives

In this lesson, students learn to look carefully for words that run together and learn to use the editor's symbol that means "put a space here."

Skills Focus

- Appreciating the value of spacing words properly in text
- Reading closely to look for words that run together
- Learning to use the editor's symbol that means "insert space here"
- Editing run-together text to correct spacing

Time Frame

Allow about 20 minutes for this lesson, excluding Setting Up the Lesson and any extensions.

Setting Up the Lesson

Text in which all the words are run together is very hard to read. You can show this to your students easily by writing them a short note in which you leave no spaces, like this: *Goodmorning studentshowiseveryonetoday?* Ask if it would be easier to read if you wrote it this way: *Good morning, students! How is everyone today?*

Explain that while most writers do not run all of their words together, it's easy to forget. Careful editors always look back over their work to see if any spaces are needed. If there are, editors use a special symbol to mark the spot that needs a space, like this: ⅄⃥

Model this symbol for your students. Then, model it again slowly, asking them to write it with you. Repeat until everyone feels comfortable. Ask them to tell you once again what it means: Put a space here.

Teaching the Lesson

No Crowding!

Invite students to look at the sample sentence. Ask them to look for any words that run together. Ask them to tell you which words run together. (*Funnydream*)

Ask them to look at the sample with the editor's mark inserted. Ask them

to practice inserting the symbol in just the right spot.

Warm Up

Ask students to go through the three sample sentences, using the "Put a space here" symbol right where it is needed. They should have inserted three symbols, like this:

1. I forgot to turn the computer ⅄⃥ off.

2. May I ⅄⃥ have a little more?

3. My ⅄⃥ team has practice on Tuesday.

Practice

Let students read the example about "My friend Gracie" on their own but remind them to look for words crowded together and to mark each spot where space is needed.

When they have finished, they should count the number of times they used the space symbol, and write that number in the blank provided.

Share with a Friend

Ask students to share their editing with a friend. Discuss results and review the paragraph about Gracie, showing where you would insert spacing symbols:

My friend Gracie spent ⅄⃥ the night on Friday. She brought a movie ⅄⃥ for us to watch. It is too ⅄⃥ rainy for us to play in ⅄⃥ the ⅄⃥ yard. We get to order a pizza ⅄⃥ and make cookies, too.

Students should have used the symbol 6 times to make all needed corrections. If no one finds all 6 on the first try, tell them how many they are looking for, and ask them to look once more, working with a partner.

Scribbles Has a Question

Ask students to discuss their thoughts. Do spaces make a difference? You bet!

A Writer's Secret

Ask how many students remember to write on every other line in case they want room to make a change or add a word? This is an important writing strategy that helps students get ready for increased revision and editing later on.

Extending the Lesson

- Ask students to write a short passage (three to five sentences) on any topic at all. Ask them to think about spacing. Encourage them to look (with partners) at the spacing. Are all the words standing by themselves? Are any words scrunched together?

- Create a short piece of text on the overhead or chalkboard in which you deliberately run some words together. HINT: Be careful not to include too many errors in any one sentence, or the task can become too challenging. Ask students to show you where to make the corrections. Ask for volunteers to model corrections for the class.

Advanced Extensions

- Look again at Scribbles' question. How many spaces does he need in this sentence? (7) Can your students identify them all?

- If your students did well with the previous challenge, invite them to create some editing lessons of their own. Ask each student to write one sentence of four to eight words. The sentences should be printed in big letters. Ask students to leave the spaces out on purpose. Then, ask them to exchange papers with partners. Partners will act as editors, using the right symbol to show where the spaces should go. NOTE: Correct spelling makes this activity much easier to tell where the spaces should go! It is fine to ask the writer to read his/her sentence aloud to help the editor make out the individual words. Repeat this activity periodically to increase students' editing skills as well as their awareness of the impact of spelling and spacing on overall readability.

Lesson 23

Capitals at the Start

For use with pages 95–98 in the *Student Traitbook.*

Many of your students probably know the importance of a capital letter to begin each sentence. Still, some may occasionally forget! The missed capital is a common error, and one every editor must learn to look for. In this lesson, students will gain some practice checking for capitals to start a sentence and using the correct editor's symbol to mark any lower case sentence beginnings that need to be capitalized.

Objectives

Students will sharpen their skills in reading like editors, spotting and correcting forgotten capitals at the beginnings of sentences.

Skills Focus

- Looking for missing capitals at the beginnings of sentences
- Learning the correct editor's symbol to change a lower case letter to a capital
- Applying this editor's symbol as needed to change a lower case letter to a capital

Time Frame

Allow about 20 minutes for this lesson, excluding Setting Up the Lesson and any extensions.

Setting Up the Lesson

When something important or interesting is about to begin, there is often a signal of some kind. See how many examples of this your students can think of. For instance, how do you know when a movie is about to start? (The theater gets darker, and the sound gets louder.) How do you know when it's time for recess at school? (There's a bell, buzzer, or other signal.) After brainstorming, mention that there is a signal for the start of a new sentence, too: the capital letter.

Read the Introduction to Lesson 23 as students follow along. Then, ask them to get ready to read like editors, using their eyes and ears.

Teaching the Lesson

Read Like an Editor

Let students read the example on their own, looking for missing capitals. They should find one, at the beginning of the second sentence.

When students have finished looking at the example, ask what they found. Most should have noticed the lower case letter "e" on the word *every*, second sentence. Ask students to notice the editor's symbol used to mark the lower case "e": a triple underscore. Show them on the chalkboard/overhead how

to make this symbol. Model it a second time, asking students to write with you. Practice until this symbol is easy for everyone to write.

Warm Up

Ask students to look for lower case letters at the beginnings of sentences. How should these be marked? Triple underscore: ≡

When they have finished, they should indicate how many times they used the symbol for changing a lower case letter to a capital. (4) Here are the corrected sample sentences:

1. when will dinner be ready?
   ≡
2. If it snows hard, we won't have school. we can play.
   ≡
3. swimming is my favorite sport. we
   ≡   ≡
   have a pool in our neighborhood.

Practice

Be sure everyone remembers the symbol for inserting a space: ⩔. You may wish to model this once more for review, and ask students to practice writing it once. Then, ask them to read and edit the paragraph. It is OK to read aloud softly. They should mark needed capitals and also mark places where a space is needed.

When they have finished, ask them to indicate how many corrections of each kind they made.

Share with a Friend

Provide time for students to share with friends. Remind them to count the number of symbols of each kind they used.

Share the corrections you have made:

walking in the rain is a lot of fun. it's

even more fun when there are lots of

puddles. I wear boots so I can jump

in every puddle. the deep puddles are

the best.

Scribbles Has a Question

Talk about the issue of mostly doing something right—but not trying to get everything right. If most of your sentences start with a capital letter, is that really good enough?

A Writer's Secret

Ask how many of your students have ever helped another student with editing. How many of them ask for help when they need it? You may wish to talk about your own experience getting help with your editing. Even experienced professional writers get help.

Extending the Lesson

- Rewrite a short paragraph from a favorite book (or other source), omitting some of the capitals at the beginnings of sentences. Make the font big and leave space for corrections. See how many errors they can find. When finding three becomes too easy, give them a sample with six or more. Be sure not to make a mistake on every sentence, though; that makes your editors' job too easy!

- Ask students to review a piece of their own writing for capitals at the beginnings of sentences. How many remembered every one? Give a small award for this.

Advanced Extensions

- Copy a sample of text from any book that makes extensive and/or creative use of capital letters. Look at the capitals with your students. How many different ways are there to use capital letters besides beginning sentences? Make a list.

- Think about where we use capitals: at sentence beginnings, on names, or to show emphasis on an important word. Have some fun pretending to be capital letters writing about themselves. Invite students to write short notes or journal entries. Is the capital letter important? Is it a necessary convention?

I Know It on Sight!

For use with pages 99–102 in the *Student Traitbook.*

Some words we sound out as we read or write, and some we just know from memory. These "sight words" are usually short—no more than four or five letters. They are important, though, because we use them so much. For this reason, readers expect them to be spelled correctly. This lesson focuses on reading closely to check the spelling of these common, frequently used words.

Objectives

Students will recognize and correct misspellings of common sight words.

Skills Focus

- Reviewing a list of eight common sight words
- Checking text for misspelled sight words
- Correcting misspellings by crossing out the wrong word and writing the correct word above it

Time Frame

Allow about 20 minutes for this lesson, excluding Setting Up the Lesson and any extensions.

Setting Up the Lesson

To set up this lesson, you need some easily recognizable photographs of your students (eight or so will do). Include a photo of yourself in the collection as well. Students can bring photos from home, or you can take snapshots (all will be returned at the close of the lesson). Shuffle the photos and place them face down at first. Then, tell students you are only going to give them a few seconds to recognize each person. Hold the photos up one at a time, giving students only a few seconds to recognize the person in the photo. If this is too easy, cut the amount of time. A second or two may be enough! Ask why it is so easy to recognize these people. Because you see them all the time! Well, some words are like that.

Read the introduction to Lesson 24 aloud as your students follow along. Ask them to get ready to check the spelling on some sight words most of them should know.

Teaching the Lesson

Read

Ask students to look carefully through the list of eight sight words. Ask how many of these are familiar to your students. How many are words they use often? (Most should be.)

Warm Up

Ask students to notice the example of the misspelled word *thay*. They should notice that it is crossed out, and the correct spelling (*they*) is written right above it. Explain that this is an easy way to correct a word that is spelled wrong. NOTE: It is not necessary to rewrite the whole sentence!

Now, ask them to practice on the example about the play. Be sure they understand that they do not need to rewrite a whole sentence—only the word or words that are misspelled.

Here is a corrected version:

I am going to a play today
with   They
~~whith~~ my parents. ~~Thay~~ say I have
~~hav~~ to dress up.

          you like
Do ~~yuw lik~~ plays?

Practice

The purpose is to extend their practice in spotting and correcting errors. Ask them to read the paragraph looking for spelling errors and correcting any that they find. HINT: There are more than five this time! (There are eight, but do not share this total just yet.)

When students finish, ask them to check their work with a partner to see if they found the same errors. Then, ask how many errors students found. Did anyone find all eight? You may wish to give an award sticker for "Good Sleuthing." This is a lot of errors for students to spot! Following is the corrected copy:

Big brothers ~~der~~ **are** a pain. I have ~~hav~~ two of them, and only ~~wun~~ **one** **like** is nice. I ~~liek~~ both of them but only one at a time. Do you have ~~eny~~ **any** brothers?

Change Hats

Ask students to choose a topic from the list of three, or to pick a writing topic of their own. When they have chosen a topic, ask them to write a short poem or paragraph using five (or more) of the sight words from the list. (You may wish to ask them to underline these sight words to make it easier to check the spelling.)

Ask them to take turns sharing their poems or paragraphs. Writers should read aloud as partners follow along and help check the spelling of sight words. Remind them to use the list as a guide to make sure the spelling is correct. How many got all the sight words they marked right? Congratulations are in order!

Scribbles Has a Question

Talk about this idea of making up your own spelling. Would it work? Why not? Can your students think of some things that would be harder (reading the paper, reading traffic signs, reading food labels) if people made up their own spelling?

A Writer's Secret

Ask how many students finish their writing first—then edit. Explain that "editing as you go" might sound like a good way to save time, but it can slow a writer down! Why? Because your brain needs to think and work as you write—and fretting over spelling and punctuation gives your brain a lot of tasks to work on all at once. So, write first. Then, review your work to look for missing punctuation, missing capitals, or misspelled words. Your writing and your editing will improve!

Extending the Lesson

- Expand your list of sight words to fifteen or so (even more if you like). Ask students to brainstorm sight words that do not appear on the list from this lesson. Make a poster you can put on the wall for easy reference. Keep expanding as the year goes on. Arrange them alphabetically for easy reference. NOTE: It's OK to "vote a word off" if no one has misspelled it for two weeks—but it can return if it pops up again!

- Do your students keep personal dictionaries? If not, this is a good time to begin! Add some of your sight words to students' personal dictionaries and continue adding new ones in the weeks to come.

Advanced Extensions

- Play "Stump the Teacher" with some spelling words your students think you should know. This is a chance for them to be the experts. Each pair of students will come up with a different common word. Write each word on an overhead list, but do not show it to the class until you are finished with the whole list of 5 or 6 words. Ask other students to take this spelling "quiz" right along with you (only those students who look up each word will know the right spelling for sure). When you have finished the list, share your words one at a time, asking the students who found the word to confirm the correct spelling. Did you get them all right? Did your students get them right?

- As you review students' work each week, keep a running list of misspelled words that come up more than once. Create a short spelling "quiz" by writing a paragraph for your students to edit, using these words. A good editing quiz of this type should have from four to eight misspelled words (you can include more if your students are ready for it). Give points this way: catch the mistake first time through—2 points per word. Catch the mistake second time through—1 point per word. (It's fine for students to check each other's work once they've gone through the paragraph individually.)

Conventions

Teacher's Guide pages 95, 189–200
Overhead numbers 21–24

Objective

Students will review and apply what they have learned about the trait of conventions.

Reviewing Conventions

Review with students what they have learned about the trait of conventions. Ask students to discuss what conventions are and to explain why conventions are important in a piece of writing. Then, ask them to recall the main points about conventions that are discussed in Unit 6. Students' responses should include the following points:

- Know the difference between statements and questions.
- Know that words need spaces between them.
- Begin each sentence with a capital.
- Correctly spell eight common words.

Applying Conventions

To help students apply what they have learned about the trait of conventions, distribute copies of the Student Rubric for Conventions on page 95 of this Teacher's Guide. Students will use these to rate one or more of the sample papers that begin on page 114. The papers for conventions are also on the overhead transparencies 21–24.

Before students look at the papers, explain that a rubric will help them determine how strong a piece of writing is for a particular trait. Preview the Student Rubric for Conventions, pointing out that a paper very strong in conventions is rated as "Made it!" and a paper very weak in conventions is rated as "It's a start." Tell students to read the rubric and then read the paper they will rate. Then, tell them to look at the paper and the rubric together to determine the rating the paper should receive. Encourage students to make notes on each paper to help them evaluate it. For example, they might use editing symbols to note a need for spaces or capital letters.

Wrap-up Activities

The wrap-up activities in this section are designed for students who have had a chance to work with all six traits of writing.

This closure section should not be thought of as a test, but as a review and a chance for you to see how far your students have come in working with the traits. We recommend doing all of the closure activities, if time permits. Each activity should take about 15 minutes.

Wrap-up Activity 1

Which Trait Is It?

For use with Student Traitbook, pages 103–104

Here, students are asked to match a description of each trait with the name of the trait. These descriptions should be simple enough that students have little difficulty making each match. However, should any confusion arise, you can refer to the appropriate trait definition in your Teacher's Guide. Also, do not hesitate to check rubrics (it is fine for students to have rubrics in front of them throughout this and all Wrap-Up activities). Take time to explain any trait students find confusing.

Teach this lesson by

- Briefly reviewing the list of six traits that appears in the Student Traitbook

- Asking students to work with partners

- Reminding students that it is OK to look at rubrics

- Reading through each description with students

- Reviewing all choices once students have finished

Answers: 1. Sentence Fluency, 2. Word Choice, 3. Conventions, 4. Ideas, 5. Organization, 6. Voice

© Great Source. Copying is prohibited.

Writing Detective

For use with Student Traitbook, pages 105–106

In this lesson, students become "writing detectives." Each of the very short samples provided has one obvious problem. The purpose of this closure lesson is to find out whether students can use what they know about the six traits to discover the main problem in each sample.

Teach this lesson by

- Asking students to work with partners

- Reminding students to look at their rubrics

- Reading each sample aloud as students read along

- Reviewing all three samples once students have finished and clarifying anything that is confusing

- Asking students to reflect briefly on how they did

Response and Rationale for Sample 1

The answer should be **FLUENCY: The writer begins every sentence the same way.** The words are clear, and the general message makes sense. The conventions are fine; there are no spelling errors. The main problem is that all the sentences begin with the word "I."

Response and Rationale for Sample 2

The answer should be **CONVENTIONS: The writing has mistakes.** "I" is not capitalized, and the sentences run together; there are no periods. Also, "ice" and "eat" are misspelled. The message is clear and the writer is actually quite enthusiastic about ice cream, saying he/she could eat it for every meal! The ideas and voice can get lost, though, when mistakes slow a reader down.

Response and Rationale for Sample 3

The answer should be **IDEAS: The writer is talking about two different topics**—going camping and getting a pet turtle. The conventions are fine, however, and sentences do begin in different ways.

Ask students to look back over the three samples. They should reflect with partners on how they did, then put a check in the right blank under **Think about It**. Student teams who found two or all three problems should consider themselves very good writing detectives! Be sure to clarify anything students find confusing.

Wrap-up Activity 3

Dear Scribbles

For use with Student Traitbook, page 106

This open-ended activity gives students a chance to share what is most memorable to them from all that they have learned. The idea is to put them in the position of being "teachers," sharing the best tips they can with Scribbles, who is having difficulty with his writing.

Set this lesson up with a quick discussion of important things you have learned together. You do not need to write these down. Just chat. Your informal discussion provides a warm-up for the notes students will write individually.

It is not necessary to put a length limit on students' notes, but encourage all students who are capable of doing so to write at least four sentences. If they can write more, so much the better! It is fine to include illustrations as well.

Sample Papers

Contents

Sample Papers: Introduction

The purpose of the Sample Papers is to help students better understand each of the six traits by seeing each one "in action." By learning to evaluate a piece of writing, students become better revisers and writers. This Sample Papers section contains copymasters of 24 Sample Papers: four for each trait. Each paper is also on an overhead transparency. For each trait, you will find two fairly strong papers and two weaker (developing or beginning) papers. The Teacher's Guide provides suggested assessments (using the primary rubrics).

Exception: The one exception to the two-strong, two-weak rule is the trait of Conventions. All papers selected to illustrate that trait have problems to give students practice in spotting, and, if you desire, correcting particular kinds of errors. Papers for all other traits have been edited, so any of them may be used to illustrate strong conventions.

Using the Sample Papers

You can use each paper alone, in which case you need to allow about 10–15 minutes. Or you can use the papers in pairs, in which case you should allow 20–30 minutes. You must decide whether your students can focus their attention for an extended discussion. If you use the papers in pairs, you will find it helpful to select one stronger paper and one developing or beginning paper for contrast. You might break this "sharing" lesson into two parts and do it on two separate days.

In advance

Read the paper aloud *to yourself* so you know it well and feel prepared to share it with students.

At the time of the lesson

- Distribute copies of the appropriate Student Rubric and Sample Paper. Remind students about key points they should be looking or listening for in response to a particular paper. This will help them connect the paper to a particular trait. Keep the list short. (Tips for each paper are given in the *Teacher's Guide.*)

- Read the paper aloud to your students, using as much inflection as the text suggests. Some papers have a lot of voice, while others have very little. Be enthusiastic, but don't try to "invent" voice where it does not exist. (1–2 minutes)

- If you use hard copies of the papers, you might ask students to perform simple tasks, such as underlining favorite words or circling overused words. Allow time for this activity before discussing the paper. (1–2 minutes)

- Have students reflect on the strengths or weaknesses of a paper while talking with a partner. (1–2 minutes)

- When partners have finished talking, discuss the paper with the whole class. Ask how many students consider the paper strong. Ask how many think it has problems. Write down strengths and problems as students share them. (1–2 minutes)

- For weaker papers, ask what a writer could do to revise. One or two suggestions is enough, for example, changing one word or deleting a word or sentence. Don't overwhelm your writers! You want them to feel in control. (1–2 minutes)

- If you wish to extend the discussion, see the Teacher's Guide for suggested questions for each paper. (3 minutes or less)

Sample Papers

IDEAS

Paper 1: My Favorite Toy (It's a start—Beginning)*

Paper 2: Frogs (Made it!—Strong)

Paper 3: The Cactus (Getting there—Developing)

Paper 4: The Fort (Made it!—Strong)

ORGANIZATION

Paper 5: The Band (It's a start—Beginning)

Paper 6: The Day We Got Our Puppy (Getting there—Developing)

Paper 7: How to Make a Salad (Made it!—Strong)

Paper 8: Catching Creatures (Made it!—Strong)

VOICE

Paper 9: Bats in the Attic (Made it!—Strong)

Paper 10: The Zoo (It's a start—Beginning)

Paper 11: The Time I Got Scared (Getting there—Developing)

Paper 12: The Meanies (Made it!—Strong)

WORD CHOICE

Paper 13: A Birthday Gift (Getting there—Developing)

Paper 14: Leprechauns (Made it!—Strong)

Paper 15: My Room (It's a start—Beginning)

Paper 16: Gross, Gross, Gross! (Made it!—Strong)

SENTENCE FLUENCY

Paper 17: Elephants (Made it!—Strong)

Paper 18: Tiny (Made it!—Strong)

Paper 19: Fun Land (It's a start—Beginning)

Paper 20: My Cat Cleo (Getting there—Developing)

CONVENTIONS

Paper 21: The Long Trip (Getting there—Developing)

Paper 22: Feeding the Chickens (Getting there—Developing)

Paper 23: Sunburn (It's a start—Beginning)

Paper 24: A Day to Remember (Getting there—Developing)

*See the Appendix, beginning on page 201, for 6-point and 5-point rubrics.

Unit 1
Ideas

Sample Paper 1: My Favorite Toy

Objectives

Students will learn that a clear main idea is key to good writing. When it is hard to identify the main idea, readers feel confused.

Materials

Student Rubric for Ideas (Teacher's Guide page 5)

Sample Paper 1: My Favorite Toy (Teacher's Guide page 120 and/or Overhead 1)

Presenting and Responding to the Paper

1. Distribute copies of the sample paper and the Student Rubric for Ideas. Use the rubric to focus students' attention on the key features of the trait of Ideas—main message and details. Review any of these concepts that your students do not understand: **main message, details, knowing the topic**.

2. Share the paper, reading aloud as students follow along. Don't hesitate to read the paper more than once during the lesson.

3. Ask students to look at their rubrics, mark their responses (individually) by putting a check in the appropriate blank, and write why they chose a particular rating.

4. Ask students to compare their responses with those of a partner. They should take a few minutes to talk about the paper and ask each other questions. Expect this process to be slow at first; they will talk more as time goes on.

5. After one or two minutes, ask for responses from the whole class. If you like, jot down some of their ideas on a separate overhead. It may be helpful to read the paper aloud a second time.

Discussing the Paper

Discuss the paper with the class. Ask students to say what ratings they gave the paper and why. The *why* is the most important part in deepening their understanding. Use the following questions to encourage class discussion:

• What is the writer's main message? Can you say it back in your own words?

• Is this paper about a toy? Is it about playing in the tub? Is it about cats?

• Do you still have questions for the writer?

Response to the Paper

This paper is at the beginning level (**It's a start.**). The writer does not describe the toy clearly. It is difficult to picture. In addition, there really is no main message; the paper is partly about the toy and partly about playing in the tub. It is not clear what the writer really wants to say. On the positive side, the writer has many possibilities for topics: the toy, playing in the tub, playing with the cat, or how baths make you wrinkly but sleepy. Developing any one topic (with text and pictures) will result in a good paper.

Extensions

1. Ask students to try drawing a picture of the toy. Then, ask them to compare their pictures. Do they look alike—or different? What does this tell us about the writer's description? Do students have to make up their own details?

2. Brainstorm a list of questions you would like to ask the writer of "My Favorite Toy." What would help you picture the toy in your mind?

3. Sometimes writers add information they do not really need. Did this writer do this? Brainstorm a list of things this writer could have left out.

Advanced Extension

Ask students to write two or three sentences about a favorite toy. They can draw a picture to go with this description. Before writing, talk about the kinds of details that make a description clear: size, color, shape, etc. Invite volunteers to read their pieces aloud without showing pictures. Can other students picture the toy in their heads just from the words?

Note: Students who have difficulty writing/reading this much text can do an oral description to go with a picture.

*See Teacher's Guide page 209 for a 6-point rubric. See page 203 for a 5-point rubric.

Sample Paper 1: IDEAS

My Favorite Toy

I like playing in water. My favorite toy can float in the tub. It is green but not too green. It has little funny marks that could be eyes. But they are *not* eyes! If I had a cat, he could play with my toy. When I take a bath, I like to stay in until my feet get wrinkly. The best time to take a bath is right before bed. You fall asleep like a rock in the road. Toys are good to have. I like cats a lot.

Think about the paper. Is the writer's main message clear? Put a check (√) in the blank that shows what you think about this paper. Then, write the reason for your rating.

___ **Made it!**

___ **Getting there . . .**

___ **It's a start.**

_____

_____

_____

Sample Paper 2: Frogs

Objective

Students will learn that interesting details help make a piece of writing strong in ideas.

Materials

Student Rubric for Ideas (Teacher's Guide page 5)

Sample Paper 2: Frogs (Teacher's Guide pages 123–124 and/or Overhead 2)

Presenting and Responding to the Paper

1. Distribute copies of the sample paper and the Student Rubric for Ideas. Use the rubric to focus students' attention on the key features of the trait of Ideas—main message and details. Review any of these concepts that your students do not understand: **main message, details, knowing the topic**.

2. Share the paper, reading aloud as students follow along. Don't hesitate to read the paper more than once during the lesson.

3. Ask students to look at their rubrics, mark their responses (individually) by putting a check in the appropriate blank, and write why they chose a particular rating.

4. Ask students to compare their responses with those of a partner. They should take a few minutes to talk about the paper and ask each other questions. Expect this process to be slow at first; they will talk more as time goes on.

5. After one or two minutes, ask for responses from the whole class. If you like, jot down some of their ideas on a separate overhead. It may be helpful to read the paper aloud a second time.

Discussing the Paper

Discuss the paper with the class. Ask students to say what ratings they gave the paper and why. The *why* is the most important part in deepening their understanding. Use the following questions to encourage class discussion:

• Does the writer's paper tell you how it might feel to be a frog?

• Is this paper easy to understand?

• What details does the writer share about a frog's life?

• Do you think you would like being a frog? Why or why not?

Response to the Paper

This paper is at the strong level (**Made it!**). The writer seems to have thought a lot about the topic and seems to know quite a bit about frogs and how they live. The details are plentiful: shiny green skin, swimming in the pond to keep cool, hiding under logs from predators, playing with other frogs, using strong legs to swim and hop, singing at night, and having to eat flies or worry about getting eaten. Also, this piece is well-focused. The writer sticks with the topic of frogs.

Extensions

1. Ask students to draw a picture of a frog based on one detail from the story. Choose a moment in the life of a frog—hiding out, eating a fly, resting in the sun, etc.

2. Invite students to write about a frog's life from the point of view of the frog. How would it feel? What might you be thinking or doing if you were a frog? Encourage students to write as much as they can, using what they know.

Advanced Extension

Does a frog have a good life? Ask students to write a persuasive piece taking one side or the other. They should back up their ideas with as many details and examples as possible. It is fine to include pictures to help illustrate main points.

* See Teacher's Guide page 209 for a 6-point rubric. See page 203 for a 5-point rubric.

Sample Paper 2: Ideas

Frogs

Would you like to be a frog? I would. If you're a frog, you have beautiful green skin that shines in the sunlight. You can swim in the pond all day to keep cool. You sit on a log and rest in the sun. You get to play with the other frogs. If anyone tries to catch you, like kids, you hide out in your secret hiding place under the logs. That way, they can't put you in a jar! If you are a frog, you have strong legs. You can leap almost as far as a cat. At night, you sing with the other frogs. This is called croaking. There is a bad part to being a frog. Frogs have to eat flies and other disgusting things. That is the only part I would not like. Plus frogs get eaten sometimes by fish or snakes. But mostly, a frog's life is very, very good.

Think about the paper. Does the writer use good details to make the message clear? Put a check (√) in the blank that shows what you think about this paper. Then, write the reason for your rating.

___ **Made it!**

___ **Getting there . . .**

___ **It's a start.**

_____

_____

_____

_____

_____

Sample Paper 3: The Cactus

Objective

Students will learn that when a writer talks about too many things at once, the main message gets buried in the jumble!

Materials

Student Rubric for Ideas (Teacher's Guide page 5)

Sample Paper 3: The Cactus (Teacher's Guide pages 127–128 and/or Overhead 3)

Presenting and Responding to the Paper

1. Distribute copies of the sample paper and the Student Rubric for Ideas. Use the rubric to focus students' attention on the key features of the trait of Ideas—main message and details. Review any of these concepts that your students do not understand: **main message, details, knowing the topic**.

2. Share the paper, reading aloud as students follow along. Don't hesitate to read the paper more than once during the lesson.

3. Ask students to look at their rubrics, mark their responses (individually) by putting a check in the appropriate blank, and write why they chose a particular rating.

4. Ask students to compare their responses with those of a partner. They should take a few minutes to talk about the paper and ask each other questions. Expect this process to be slow at first; they will talk more as time goes on.

5. After one or two minutes, ask for responses from the whole class. If you like, jot down some of their ideas on a separate overhead. It may be helpful to read the paper aloud a second time.

Discussing the Paper

Discuss the paper with the class. Ask students to say what ratings they gave the paper and why. The *why* is the most important part in deepening their understanding. Use the following questions to encourage class discussion:

• Does the writer tell you a lot about the cactus plant?

• Does the writer talk mainly about the cactus or about many things?

• Is it confusing when writers talk about too many things in one paper?

Response to the Paper

This paper is at a mid-point level (**Getting there . . .**). The writer seems to know quite a bit about the cactus—it is prickly, it does not need much water—and shares several interesting details. In the second part of the paper, though, the writer begins telling about several other topics (the kangaroo rat, the tortoise) and seems to forget about the cactus—the main topic of the paper. The writer could talk more about animals of the desert or else stick with the cactus and keep other topics for next time.

Extensions

1. Ask students to try crossing out everything in the paper that is not about the cactus. How much is left? What does this tell us about the writing? Is it about one thing (the cactus) or many things?

2. Brainstorm other things your students know about the cactus plant. Use one, two, or more of these details to expand the cactus paper.

Advanced Extension

Use a list or word web to brainstorm ideas on any place (like the desert) or animal (like the kangaroo rat or tortoise). Students should be free to select their own personally important topics (but they need to be small and focused—not "the earth" or "plants"). Ask students to write a paragraph of four sentences or more, sharing details on this topic. Tell them, "In this paper, tell your reader about one main thing. Don't try to tell about too many things." Share some results aloud. Talk about how having one main message makes writing clear and easy to understand.

* See Teacher's Guide page 209 for a 6-point rubric. See page 203 for a 5-point rubric.

name: .... date: ....

Sample Paper 3: Ideas

The Cactus

We have about 100 plants at our house! My mom loves plants! But one kind of plant can grow without much water. It is the cactus. A cactus has prickly spears called thorns. It can live in the desert. The desert is hot and dry almost all the time. It can get to over 100 degrees. A cactus does not mind a lot of heat. It keeps right on growing! Some animals can live in the desert. A special rat called the kangaroo rat lives there. They hop very fast across the sand so they do not burn their feet. I saw a tortoise once when we drove through the desert. It was right on the highway. I wanted to take it home! My dad said it needed to stay in its desert home.

name: .... date: ....

Think about the paper. Does the writer seem to know a lot about the cactus? Does the writer *mostly* tell about the cactus or about other things? Put a check (√) in the blank that shows what you think about this paper. Then, write the reason for your rating.

___ **Made it!**

___ **Getting there . . .**

___ **It's a start.**

_____

_____

_____

_____

_____

_____

Sample Paper 4: The Fort

Objective

Students will learn that when a writer knows a lot about the topic, the writing tends to be strong.

Materials

Student Rubric for Ideas (Teacher's Guide page 5)

Sample Paper 4: The cactus (Teacher's Guide pages 131–132 and/or Overhead 4)

Presenting and Responding to the Paper

1. Distribute copies of the sample paper and the Student Rubric for Ideas. Use the rubric to focus students' attention on the key features of the trait of Ideas—main message and details. Review any of these concepts that your students do not understand: **main message, details, knowing the topic**.

2. Share the paper, reading aloud as students follow along. Don't hesitate to read the paper more than once during the lesson.

3. Ask students to look at their rubrics, mark their responses (individually) by putting a check in the appropriate blank, and write why they chose a particular rating.

4. Ask students to compare their responses with those of a partner. They should take a few minutes to talk about the paper and ask each other questions. Expect this process to be slow at first; they will talk more as time goes on.

5. After one or two minutes, ask for responses from the whole class. If you like, jot down some of their ideas on a separate overhead. It may be helpful to read the paper aloud a second time.

Discussing the Paper

Discuss the paper with the class. Ask students to say what ratings they gave the paper and why. The *why* is the most important part in deepening their understanding. Use the following questions to encourage class discussion:

• Does the writer know a lot about building forts? How can you tell?

• The writer says the branches of the oak tree were like arms holding up the fort. Do you like this detail? Why or why not? What other details do you like?

• Do good details show that a writer knows a lot about the topic? Why?

Response to the Paper

This paper is at a **Made it!** level. The writer seems to have thought a lot about the fort and shares a lot of information about the fort and his/her experiences there. The writing is clear and easy to understand. It is focused, with rich detail, so the fort is easy to see in our minds. This writer knows the topic well.

Extensions

• Ask students to draw a picture of a fort that they would like to have. Share pictures and talk about the kinds of details each artist/writer put in his/her picture.

• Have your students ever built a fort? Talk a little about fort-building adventures. Then, ask students to write a short paragraph (3–5 sentences) about one adventure building or playing in a fort. Tell them that it's okay to make up a story if they have not done this!

Advanced Extension

A fort is one special kind of place. Talk about why: it's a place you build yourself, it's a place where you hang out with friends, and it's a place where you can be alone when you feel like it. Ask students to think of another place that is special to them—any place at all. Then, ask them to brainstorm all the things they can think of to describe the place—how it looks, smells, sounds, and feels like to be there. They can use these details to write a short descriptive paragraph or poem. Share results, or if you like, create a class book.

* See Teacher's Guide page 209 for a 6-point rubric. See page 203 for a 5-point rubric.

Sample Paper 4: IDEAS

The Fort

About a year ago, my friend and I build a fort. It was high in a huge old oak tree with branches like arms. The arms held us up. The fort took a long time to build. We kept adding to it. It finally got big enough to lie down in. It was open on the sides and it had a door. The door was in the floor! You could climb up using a rope ladder. My dog could not climb the ladder so I carried him up. When you climbed up, you could see over the roof of our house. We took food up there. We also took a radio. My mom gave us a fuzzy red rug for the floor. We would sit and look out or listen to music. Our roof was strong and kept out most of the rain. It was the only fort like it. My mom was always afraid we would fall out, but we never did.

Think about the paper. Does the writer seem to know a lot about forts? Does the writer tell enough so you can picture the fort? Put a check (√) in the blank that shows what you think about this paper. Then, write the reason for your rating.

___ **Made it!**

___ **Getting there . . .**

___ **It's a start.**

_____

_____

_____

_____

_____

_____

Unit 2

Organization

Sample Paper 5: The Band

Objective

Students will learn that when a writer wanders from one topic to another, it is hard for readers to follow.

Materials

Student Rubric for Organization (Teacher's Guide page 23)

Sample Paper 5: The Band (Teacher's Guide page 135 and/or Overhead 5)

Presenting and Responding to the Paper

1. Distribute copies of the sample paper and the Student Rubric for Organization. Use the rubric to focus students' attention on the key features of the trait of Organization— having a good beginning and ending, keeping things in order, and not wandering from the main topic. Review any of these concepts that your students do not understand: **beginning, ending, order, wandering**.

2. Share the paper, reading aloud as students follow along. Don't hesitate to read the paper more than once during the lesson.

3. Ask students to look at their rubrics, mark their responses (individually) by putting a check in the appropriate blank, and write why they chose a particular rating.

4. Ask students to compare their responses with those of a partner. They should take a few minutes to talk about the paper and ask each other questions. Expect this process to be slow at first; they will talk more as time goes on.

5. After one or two minutes, ask for responses from the whole class. If you like, jot down some of their ideas on a separate overhead. It may be helpful to read the paper aloud a second time.

Discussing the Paper

Discuss the paper with the class. Ask students to say what ratings they gave the paper and why. The *why* is the most important part in deepening their understanding. Use the following questions to encourage class discussion:

• Is the paper easy to follow?

• What is the main topic?

• Does the writer wander from the main topic?

• Is it confusing when a writer does not stick to the main topic?

Response to the Paper

This paper is at the beginning level (**It's a start.**). The title and the first line suggest that the main topic is playing jazz with the band. However, the writer wanders a lot: from the radio, to sitting in the back seat, to eating ice cream. This makes the paper hard to follow. Also, the paper has no real ending. It just stops.

Extensions

1. Ask students to try crossing out everything in the paper that is not about playing jazz in the band. What does this tell us about how much the writer wanders?

2. Show the concept of "wandering" visually. Make a straight line on the floor using a piece of masking tape. Then, ask a student volunteer to walk down that line without going off. Explain that this is like sticking with your main topic. Now, ask the student to walk the line again. This time the student will do it as you read "The Band." Each time the paper goes off the main topic, the student should "wander" from the main line. If the writer comes back, the student should come back. Other students can encourage the "writer" to stay on line, or to go off, depending on what the paper says. When you finish, talk about how students knew the paper was getting "off track."

Advanced Extension

Music inspires many writers. Play a piece of music for your class. What does the music make them think of? Make a list. From this list, ask students to pick one idea—perhaps a feeling, a place, a person, or an adventure they have had. Have students write a short paragraph (3–5 sentences or more) or a short poem (about 6 to 8 lines). Then, have them share their work. How many students were able to stick with their topic all the way through?

* See Teacher's Guide page 210 for a 6-point rubric. See page 204 for a 5-point rubric.

Sample Paper 5: Organization
The Band

I can play jazz with the band. I play the drums. Do you like music? I do! I play the radio in our car so loud it hurts my mom's ears. Then she makes me turn it down. I don't like sitting in the back seat. You can't see anything. Sometimes when we are driving we stop for ice cream. Next year, I am going to play in the band at school. I will be in third grade. We are going to do harder math.

Think about the paper. What is this writer's main topic? Does the writer stick with this topic or wander? Put a check (√) in the blank that shows what you think about this paper. Then, write the reason for your rating.

____ **Made it!**

____ **Getting there . . .**

____ **It's a start.**

_____

_____

Sample Paper 6: The Day We Got Our Puppy

Objective

Students will learn that when things are told out of order, readers get confused.

Materials

Student Rubric for Organization (Teacher's Guide page 23)

Sample Paper 6: The Day We Got Our Puppy (Teacher's Guide page 138 and/or Overhead 6)

Presenting and Responding to the Paper

1. Distribute copies of the sample paper and the Student Rubric for Organization. Use the rubric to focus students' attention on the key features of the trait of Organization— having a good beginning and ending, keeping things in order, and not wandering from the main topic. Review any of these concepts that your students do not understand: **beginning, ending, order, wandering**.

2. Share the paper, reading aloud as students follow along. Don't hesitate to read the paper more than once during the lesson.

3. Ask students to look at their rubrics, mark their responses (individually) by putting a check in the appropriate blank, and write why they chose a particular rating.

4. Ask students to compare their responses with those of a partner. They should take a few minutes to talk about the paper and ask each other questions. Expect this process to be slow at first; they will talk more as time goes on.

5. After one or two minutes, ask for responses from the whole class. If you like, jot down some of their ideas on a separate overhead. It may be helpful to read the paper aloud a second time.

Discussing the Paper

Discuss the paper with the class. Ask students to say what ratings they gave the paper and why. The *why* is the most important part in deepening their understanding. Use the following questions to encourage class discussion:

• Does the writer tell things in order? Why do you think so?

• Would you tell things in a different order?

• Is it confusing when writers jump around?

Response to the Paper

This paper is at a mid-point level (**Getting there . . .**). The writer sticks with her topic (the new puppy, Tuesday), but tells things in a confusing order. We can tell what happened, but we have to put the order together in our heads, like a puzzle. If she started with wishing for a dog, then told about the trip to the pet store, naming the dog Tuesday, and finally playing in the snow, this story would be easier to follow.

Extensions

1. Talk about which sentence in the paper should come *first*. Do your students all agree? Could more than one sentence come first?

2. Talk about which sentence should come *last* and why. Do your students all agree? Could more than one sentence go last?

Advanced Extension

Ask students to retell the story about Tuesday in order as you write it down. Then, check the order to see that their version makes sense.

* See Teacher's Guide page 210 for a 6-point rubric. See page 204 for a 5-point rubric.

Sample Paper 6: Organization

The Day We Got Our Puppy

The day we got our puppy was a Tuesday. I did not know we were getting a puppy. It was snowing hard when we got Tuesday. She eats a lot! I love her so, so much! We named her Tuesday because we got her on a Tuesday. We play with her all the time. We did not know until we got to the store we were getting a puppy. One day, my mom took us shopping. When we got home, we all played in the snow. I had a goldfish, but I wanted a dog!

Think about the paper. Does the writer tell things in order? Would you tell things in a different order? Put a check (√) in the blank that shows what you think about this paper:

___ **Made it!**

___ **Getting there . . .**

___ **It's a start.**

Sample Paper 7: How to Make a Salad

Objective

Students will learn that when a writer tells things in a clear order, the paper is easy to follow and understand.

Materials

Student Rubric for Organization (Teacher's Guide page 23)

Sample Paper 7: How to Make a Salad (Teacher's Guide pages 141–142 and/or Overhead 7)

Presenting and Responding to the Paper

1. Distribute copies of the sample paper and the Student Rubric for Organization. Use the rubric to focus students' attention on the key features of the trait of Organization—having a good beginning and ending, keeping things in order, and not wandering from the main topic. Review any of these concepts that your students do not understand: **beginning, ending, order, wandering**.

2. Share the paper, reading aloud as students follow along. Don't hesitate to read the paper more than once during the lesson.

3. Ask students to look at their rubrics, mark their responses (individually) by putting a check in the appropriate blank, and write why they chose a particular rating.

4. Ask students to compare their responses with those of a partner. They should take a few minutes to talk about the paper and ask each other questions. Expect this process to be slow at first; they will talk more as time goes on.

5. After one or two minutes, ask for responses from the whole class. If you like, jot down some of their ideas on a separate overhead. It may be helpful to read the paper aloud a second time.

Discussing the Paper

Discuss the paper with the class. Ask students to say what ratings they gave the paper and why. The *why* is the most important part in deepening their understanding. Use the following questions to encourage class discussion:

• Does this paper have a good beginning? [Read it again.] Why?

• Does the paper have a good ending? [Read it again.] Why?

• Could you follow these directions if you were really making a salad?

• Was there anything confusing in this paper? If so, what?

Response to the Paper

This paper is at the strong level (**Made it!**). The writer has a good beginning and ending and gives the reader each step in an order that makes sense. She/he starts with the lettuce and ends with the dressing and pepper—then serving the salad. It would be easy to use these directions in actually making a salad.

Extensions

1. Think of a simple process that people do often: fixing cereal, tying your shoes, feeding a pet, or brushing your teeth. As a class, brainstorm the steps required to do this process. Be sure to include all the steps, and be sure to put them in order. Move things around if you need to!

2. This writer has a pretty strong beginning to her paper. What about other writers? Ask your students to randomly choose some books from your classroom. Read the beginnings of each book. Ask students which ones they like best. If students have not yet read (or heard) some of the books, use these beginnings to predict what the books might be about.

Advanced Extension

Invite students to create a how-to paper or a recipe. Remind them to think about a strong beginning and ending and about putting all details in order. Share results with the class as a whole. Write with them and share your paper as well.

* See Teacher's Guide page 210 for a 6-point rubric. See page 204 for a 5-point rubric.

name: .... date: ....

Sample Paper 7: Organization

How to Make a Salad

Do you want to make a good salad? I will tell you how. First, ask yourself: What do I like in my salad? Everyone likes lettuce, so start with lettuce. Put in a lot. Make the leaves small so they fit in your mouth. Tear them. Do not cut them with a knife or they will turn brown. Now slice some tomatoes. Next, slice some cucumbers. You can add radishes if you like spicy food! You can even put in some mushrooms if you like. If I were you, I wouldn't bother. Mushrooms look nice, but they feel funny in your mouth, like little blobs of rubber. Pour your favorite dressing on top. Toss the salad so everything is mixed up. If you don't, the dressing will just sit on the top. I put on plenty of pepper, too. Now serve your delicious salad!

Think about the paper. Does the writer tell all the steps you need to know to make a salad? Are they in order? Put a check (√) in the blank that shows what you think about this paper. Then, write the reason for your rating.

___ **Made it!**

___ **Getting there . . .**

___ **It's a start.**

_____

_____

_____

_____

_____

_____

Sample Paper 8: Catching Creatures

Objective

Students will learn that a good beginning and ending, along with logical order, make organization stronger.

Materials

Student Rubric for Organization (Teacher's Guide page 23)

Sample Paper 8: Catching Creatures (Teacher's Guide page 145 and/or Overhead 8)

Presenting and Responding to the Paper

1. Distribute copies of the sample paper and the Student Rubric for Organization. Use the rubric to focus students' attention on the key features of the trait of Organization—having a good beginning and ending, keeping things in order, and not wandering from the main topic. Review any of these concepts that your students do not understand: **beginning, ending, order, wandering**.

2. Share the paper, reading aloud as students follow along. Don't hesitate to read the paper more than once during the lesson.

3. Ask students to look at their rubrics, mark their responses (individually) by putting a check in the appropriate blank, and write why they chose a particular rating.

4. Ask students to compare their responses with those of a partner. They should take a few minutes to talk about the paper and ask each other questions. Expect this process to be slow at first; they will talk more as time goes on.

5. After one or two minutes, ask for responses from the whole class. If you like, jot down some of their ideas on a separate overhead. It may be helpful to read the paper aloud a second time.

Discussing the Paper

Discuss the paper with the class. Ask students to say what ratings they gave the paper and why. The *why* is the most important part in deepening their understanding. Use the following questions to encourage class discussion:

- Do you like the beginning of this paper? [Read the lead again.] Why?
- Do you like the ending? [Read the ending again.] Why?
- Do any parts seem out of order?
- Does this writer ever wander from the main topic? [Read the paper again, if necessary.] If so, where?

Response to the Paper

This paper is at a strong level (**Made it!**). The beginning and ending are particularly strong, and these help keep the reader focused on the main topic of catching creatures. The body of the paper is orderly. The writer progresses from catching the creatures to the kinds of creatures you can capture, how they are different from other "pets," how it's fun to study them, and finally, why you cannot keep them too long. The piece is easy to follow.

Extensions

1. Compare the writer's actual lead to this one: *This will be a paper about creatures.* Talk about which beginning your students prefer and why. (Do not be afraid to share your opinion, and let students know you like the writer's version because it is original.)

2. Compare the writer's actual ending to this one: *Now you know some things about catching creatures.* Talk about which ending your students like better and why. (Again, share your personal opinion and your reasons.)

Advanced Extension

Invite students to write a short paragraph (about 3–6 sentences) about an unusual pet. It could be their pet or someone else's. Work hard on leads and endings. When students finish writing, ask them to underline the lead and the ending. Is each one original or one they have heard before? If it is not original, ask them to try one more time. Share results aloud. Write with them, creating two possible leads and two possible endings for your paragraph. Then, ask students to help you choose the one that works better.

* See Teacher's Guide page 210 for a 6-point rubric. See page 204 for a 5-page rubric.

Sample Paper 8: Organization

Catching Creatures

To catch creatures, you have to be fast and very quiet. That way, you don't scare them. One day I caught a praying mantis in a jar. Another day I caught a dragonfly. A pet you keep in a jar is not like a dog or cat. You can't really pet it or play with it. But a creature is still your pet. You can study it to see what it eats and how it moves. You can show it to your friends. You can't keep it too long, though or it could die. Think about it. You would not want to live in a jar!

Think about the paper. Does it begin in an interesting way? Does it end in an interesting way? Put a check (√) in the blank that shows what you think about this paper.

___ **Made it!**

___ **Getting there . . .**

___ **It's a start.**

Unit 3
Voice

Sample Paper 9: Bats in the Attic

Objectives

Students will learn that lively writing that is full of feelings makes for strong voice.

Materials

Student Rubric for Voice (Teacher's Guide page 41)

Sample Paper 9: Bats in the Attic (Teacher's Guide pages 148–149 and/or Overheads 9 and 9a)

Presenting and Responding to the Paper

1. Distribute copies of the sample paper and the Student Rubric for Voice. Use the rubric to focus students' attention on the key features of the trait of Voice—writing in a lively way, showing feelings, writing in a way that sounds like you. Review any of these concepts that your students do not understand: **talking to the reader, lively writing, showing feelings**.

2. Share the paper, reading aloud as students follow along. Don't hesitate to read the paper more than once during the lesson.

3. Ask students to look at their rubrics, mark their responses (individually) by putting a check in the appropriate blank, and write why they chose a particular rating.

4. Ask students to compare their responses with those of a partner. They should take a few minutes to talk about the paper and ask each other questions. Expect this process to be slow at first; they will talk more as time goes on.

5. After one or two minutes, ask for responses from the whole class. If you like, jot down some of their ideas on a separate overhead. It may be helpful to read the paper aloud a second time.

Discussing the Paper

Discuss the paper with the class. Ask students to say what ratings they gave the paper and why. The *why* is the most important part in deepening their understanding. Use the following questions to encourage class discussion:

- Would you describe this paper as lively? Or does the writer sound bored? (Most students should say lively.)

- What do you think this writer is like? (As you discuss this, explain that when the voice is strong, it's almost like the writer is talking to us.)

- How does this writer feel about bats? How do you know?

Response to the Paper

This paper is at a strong level (**Made it!**). The writer seems fully engaged with the topic and seems to delight in telling all about her/his horrible experience. The writer is extremely honest about his/her feelings, sharing details about the smell of the house, the creepy noises, the difficulty of getting the bats out, and the ugly faces—they might look that way because they smell bad! The whole piece has a very conversational sound, as if the writer is talking right to us. It is personal. We can easily tell how the writer feels—horrified!

Extensions

1. Ask students to create a picture showing the face of one of the bats as it left the attic. Talk about ways to put voice into pictures as well as into writing.

2. This writer seems to have a real conversation with us about the bats. What if we could write back and tell the writer what we think? Invite your students to do just that. Write a short note—and give the writer a name.

Advanced Extension

Brainstorm some bad experiences your students have had—e.g., getting stuck in a storm, getting lost, being bitten by an animal, losing a shoe. You can provide guidance on topics, and share some possible topics of your own. Then, write a short paragraph (5–7 sentences) about the experience. Encourage students to think of their readers. Write to someone in particular, such as a friend or a relative (or to you). Encourage them to think about their feelings. How do they feel about the experience? How do they want the reader to feel? Read results aloud (including yours!) to see if the feelings come through.

* See the Teacher's Guide page 211 for a 6-point rubric. See page 205 for a 5-point rubric.

Sample Paper 9: Voice

Bats in the Attic

The worst thing that happened to me was when we got bats in our attic. First, we heard these creepy sounds. We did not know what it was. My dad told us not to worry—the sound would go away. Well, it didn't! It got louder and louder till we could barely sleep. Then the whole house smelled. We could not, and I mean not, eat. Bats are very stinky, and I am not kidding. Just imagine the worst smell you have ever smelled. Well, this was ten times worse than that! The bats got in through a teeny crack below our roof. Then they hung out there. Ha, ha. They really did hang upside down! The exterminators had to come. They had to shovel bat droppings out and clean our attic. I held my nose the whole time! How would you like that job? They wore gloves to catch the bats. That way, they would not get bitten. The bats looked really mad when they had to move! But I think that is just how bats look. Maybe they are mad because they smell so awful!

Think about the paper. Does the writer have a good time telling us about the bats? Did you like listening to the paper? Put a check (√) in the blank that shows what you think about this paper. Then, write a reason for your rating.

___ **Made it!**

___ **Getting there . . .**

___ **It's a start.**

_____

_____

_____

_____

_____

Sample Paper 10: The Zoo

Objective

Students will learn that when a writer is not excited about his or her topic, the voice is weak.

Materials

Student Rubric for Voice (Teacher's Guide page 41)

Sample Paper 10: The Zoo (Teacher's Guide page 152 and/or Overhead 10)

Presenting and Responding to the Paper

1. Distribute copies of the sample paper and the Student Rubric for Voice. Use the rubric to focus students' attention on the key features of the trait of Voice—writing in a lively way, showing feelings, writing in a way that sounds like you. Review any of these concepts that your students do not understand: **talking to the reader, lively writing, showing feelings**.

2. Share the paper, reading aloud as students follow along. Don't hesitate to read the paper more than once during the lesson.

3. Ask students to look at their rubrics, mark their responses (individually) by putting a check in the appropriate blank, and write why they chose a particular rating.

4. Ask students to compare their responses with those of a partner. They should take a few minutes to talk about the paper and ask each other questions. Expect this process to be slow at first; they will talk more as time goes on.

5. After one or two minutes, ask for responses from the whole class. If you like, jot down some of their ideas on a separate overhead. It may be helpful to read the paper aloud a second time.

Discussing the Paper

Discuss the paper with the class. Ask students to say what ratings they gave the paper and why. The *why* is the most important part in deepening their understanding. Use the following questions to encourage class discussion:

• Does the writer seem excited about going to the zoo? How can you tell?

• How does this writer feel? How do you know?

• Do you feel like the writer is talking right to you? Why or why not?

Response to the Paper

This paper is at a beginning level (**It's a start.**). The writer seems bored with the topic, even though there is a lot to write about. For example, consider the mother gorilla hiding her baby from the crowd of humans. This is a good opportunity for sharing feelings, but the writer does not say much. It is hard to tell what the writer is feeling. He/she seems to be writing mainly to get something on paper. The paper is clear and organized. It just does not have much voice.

Extensions

1. Ask students to listen as you read the paper again. Then, ask if there is anything the writer could have added to make the paper more exciting, for example, more details about the baby gorilla's behavior. If your students think of more than one or two possibilities, make a list.

2. Can you picture the writer? Part of the magic of voice is that it makes us feel as if we know the writer a little bit. What expression do you picture on this writer's face as he/she is writing? Is the writer smiling, laughing, or just looking bored? Ask students to mimic that expression—then to look at one another's faces. What do they see? Follow up by drawing a picture of the writer with this expression—writing or holding the cotton candy.

Advanced Extension

What if you had been at the zoo that day and seen the baby gorilla? Could you have written with more voice? Ask students to think of a time when they saw or held a baby animal (or a human baby). Ask them to write a short paragraph (6–8 lines), putting in as much voice and feeling as possible. What expressions did they have on their faces? Encourage students to write with those same expressions to capture all the feelings they can.

* See Teacher's Guide page 211 for a 6-point rubric. See page 205 for a 5-point rubric.

Sample Paper 10: Voice

The Zoo

At the zoo we saw a gorilla. It was pretty big. It was shy and it stayed behind some rocks. The mother gorilla had a baby that she carried with her. The baby was small. We did not get to see it very well because she hid it. What do gorillas eat? I am not sure. I think they like fruit. I tried to take a picture. It was hard because they were so far away. My uncle took a picture of me holding some cotton candy. In the picture, you can see one of the gorillas.

Think about the paper. Does the writer seem excited about visiting the zoo? Can you tell how this writer is feeling? Put a check (√) in the blank that shows what you think about this paper:

____ **Made it!**

____ **Getting there . . .**

____ **It's a start.**

Sample Paper 11: The Time I Got Scared

Objective

Students will learn that the topic alone does not create voice. The writer needs to put feelings and life into the writing.

Materials

Student Rubric for Voice (Teacher's Guide page 41)

Sample Paper 11: The Time I Got Scared (Teacher's Guide pages 155–156 and/or Overhead 11)

Presenting and Responding to the Paper

1. Distribute copies of the sample paper and the Student Rubric for Voice. Use the rubric to focus students' attention on the key features of the trait of Voice—writing in a lively way, showing feelings, writing in a way that sounds like you. Review any of these concepts that your students do not understand: **talking to the reader, lively writing, showing feelings**.

2. Share the paper, reading aloud as students follow along. Don't hesitate to read the paper more than once during the lesson.

3. Ask students to look at their rubrics, mark their responses (individually) by putting a check in the appropriate blank, and write why they chose a particular rating.

4. Ask students to compare their responses with those of a partner. They should take a few minutes to talk about the paper and ask each other questions. Expect this process to be slow at first; they will talk more as time goes on.

5. After one or two minutes, ask for responses from the whole class. If you like, jot down some of their ideas on a separate overhead. It may be helpful to read the paper aloud a second time.

Discussing the Paper

Discuss the paper with the class. Ask students to say what ratings they gave the paper and why. The *why* is the most important part in deepening their understanding. Use the following questions to encourage class discussion:

• Does the writer seem scared in this paper? Why or why not?

• How does the writer feel? How can you tell?

• The writer talks about some scary things, like strange sounds and a snake in the tent. Does this make the paper scary? Why or why not?

Response to the Paper

This paper is at a mid-point level (**Getting there . . .**). The writer has chosen a scary experience to write about but does not really create a scary mood. The part about strange sounds and ghosts comes right to the edge of being scary, but the writer says it in a quiet way. This is also true of the part about the snake. It was not poisonous, but how did they know? We don't get to see or hear the kids' responses. If the writer shared more of his/her feelings, we might feel scared, too!

Extensions

1. What do you think the other kids in the tent said when they heard the strange sounds outside? Write down some things they could have said, and add those voices to the story. Read it again, and see if hearing people speak adds voice. (It should!)

2. Brainstorm things kids might have said when they first noticed a snake in the tent. Add those bits of dialogue. Then, read it again. Now how much voice does the piece have?

3. When Jake said he could hear an owl in the trees, what do you suppose the writer was thinking? Brainstorm some possibilities, and then choose one with voice and replace the last line. What does this do for the voice?

Advanced Extension

Ask students to do a role-play. Imagine they are one of the other kids in the tent that night. Ask them to write about the same experience from their point of view. What were they thinking? What were they hearing? How did it feel? Read some results aloud.

* See Teacher's Guide page 211 for a 6-point rubric. See page 205 for a 5-point rubric.

Sample Paper 11: Voice

The Time I Got Scared

A time I got scared was when I went camping last year. I went with some of my friends. We put up a tent for four of us to sleep in. In the night, we heard some strange sounds. We thought it was ghosts. Then we thought it was a bear. We never did find out what it was. We were scared to go outside. Later, a snake got into our tent. He went in my friend Jake's sleeping bag. He was not poisonous. We did not want him to bite us, so we put him outside. Jake said he could hear an owl in the trees, but I never did hear it. Where we camp there is a lake and a creek. It was fun and scary! I hope we go back.

Think about the paper. Does the writer seem scared? Do you think this is a scary paper? Put a check (√) in the blank that shows what you think about this paper. Then, write a reason for your rating.

_____ **Made it!**

_____ **Getting there . . .**

_____ **It's a start.**

_____

_____

_____

_____

_____

_____

Sample Paper 12: The Meanies

Objective

Students will learn that when a writer is honest and open about his/her feelings, the voice comes through loud and clear.

Materials

Student Rubric for Voice (Teacher's Guide page 41)

Sample Paper 12: The Meanies (Teacher's Guide pages 159–160 and/or Overhead 12)

Presenting and Responding to the Paper

1. Distribute copies of the sample paper and the Student Rubric for Voice. Use the rubric to focus students' attention on the key features of the trait of Voice—writing in a lively way, showing feelings, writing in a way that sounds like you. Review any of these concepts that your students do not understand: **talking to the reader, lively writing, showing feelings**.

2. Share the paper, reading aloud as students follow along. Don't hesitate to read the paper more than once during the lesson.

3. Ask students to look at their rubrics, mark their responses (individually) by putting a check in the appropriate blank, and write why they chose a particular rating.

4. Ask students to compare their responses with those of a partner. They should take a few minutes to talk about the paper and ask each other questions. Expect this process to be slow at first; they will talk more as time goes on.

5. After one or two minutes, ask for responses from the whole class. If you like, jot down some of their ideas on a separate overhead. It may be helpful to read the paper aloud a second time.

Discussing the Paper

Discuss the paper with the class. Ask students to say what ratings they gave the paper and why. The *why* is the most important part in deepening their understanding. Use the following questions to encourage class discussion:

• Can you tell how this writer feels?

• Is the writer honest about her feelings? Does this add to the voice? (Most students should say yes.)

• Can you tell what the writer is like by the way she writes? What is a good word to describe her? (*upset, angry, mad, hurt,* etc.)

• Does the writer ever sound bored? Does this make a difference in the voice? (Most students should say *yes.*)

Response to the Paper

This paper is at a strong level (**Made it!**). The writer is very honest about her feelings. She is exasperated, frustrated—and downright mad! She tells specific things the "meanies" have done—putting worms in her lunch box, pestering her, stealing her lunch. Then, she tells exactly how she feels about the situation in colorful terms—she wants to scream till she turns bright purple! Plus, she wishes she never had to see them again. Her strong feelings give this piece lots of life, lots of voice.

Extensions

1. What do you think a "meanie" looks like? Draw a picture of one! Then, share pictures, and talk about the voice in the pictures.

2. What if this writer had written the following? *Some people are mean. They can be mean on the playground. They say and do mean things. I hate it when they do that! I try to ignore them, but it doesn't seem to work.*

   What does this change do to the voice? Can you explain the difference? Reread the original to make the comparison easier, and see how many differences your students can come up with.

Advanced Extension

Ask students to write a short note to the author of "The Meanies." In the note, they could tell her about a similar experience they've had, or make a suggestion for dealing with the "meanies."

* See Teacher's Guide page 211 for a 6-point rubric. See page 205 for a 5-page rubric.

Sample Paper 12: Voice
The Meanies

Do you know what I hate? The playground meanies! That is my name for them. I made it up and it fits. Meanies are mean people who pester you or steal your lunch. Sometimes they put things in my lunch that nobody wants to eat, like old mooshy leaves or worms. How do you think you would like that? Then they laugh. Ha, ha. Very funny, I am sure. I feel like screaming until I turn bright purple. I tell my teacher, but she is never looking when they are doing stuff. It is not fair! My dad says to pretend that I don't see them. I have tried, but I just can't do it. I see them every single minute. I wish I would not see them for days and days and days. But they are not exactly invisible, you know!

Think about the paper. Does the writer have strong feelings? Can you tell how the writer is feeling and thinking? Put a check (√) in the blank that shows what you think about this paper. Then, write the reason for your rating.

___ **Made it!**

___ **Getting there . . .**

___ **It's a start.**

_____

_____

_____

_____

_____

_____

Unit 4

Word Choice

Sample 13: A Birthday Gift

Objective

Students will learn that even a few strong verbs make word choice stronger—but original, fresh words are needed to paint a clear picture in a reader's mind.

Materials

Student Rubric for Word Choice (Teacher's Guide page 59)
Sample Paper 13: A Birthday Gift (Teacher's Guide pages 163–164 and/or Overhead 13)

Presenting and Responding to the Paper

1. Distribute copies of the sample paper and the Student Rubric for Word Choice. Use the rubric to focus students' attention on the key features of the trait of Word Choice—using words that paint a vivid picture in the reader's mind, avoiding repetition, using strong verbs, stretching for new words. Review any of these concepts that your students do not understand: **words that help you picture things, repetition, strong verbs, stretching**.

2. Share the paper, reading aloud as students follow along. Don't hesitate to read the paper more than once during the lesson.

3. Ask students to look at their rubrics, mark their responses (individually) by putting a check in the appropriate blank, and write why they chose a particular rating.

4. Ask students to compare their responses with those of a partner. They should take a few minutes to talk about the paper and ask each other questions. Expect this process to be slow at first; they will talk more as time goes on.

5. After one or two minutes, ask for responses from the whole class. If you like, jot down some of their ideas on a separate overhead. It may be helpful to read the paper aloud a second time.

Discussing the Paper

Discuss the paper with the class. Ask students to say what ratings they gave the paper and why. The *why* is the most important part in deepening their understanding. Use the following questions to encourage class discussion.

• Verbs are action words. Do you see or hear any strong verbs in this paper?

• Do you have any favorite words? (Read the paper again, if necessary.)

• Were any words repeated?

• Is there anything you would say differently?

Response to the Paper

This paper is at a mid-point level (**Getting there**...). The writer uses some strong verbs: *weighed, carry, felt, wondered*. More would add extra energy! A few words are repeated—e.g., *good*. This is not a real problem. The language is clear, and the paper has one or two striking phrases: *round and smooth* and *I was stuffed*. Again, if the writer stretched *just* a little more, this would be a **Made it!** paper.

Extensions

1. Ask students, working with partners, to underline as many verbs as they can find. They should find at least six. Are they powerful? Medium-strength? Or weak? (We vote for medium-strength. They do not suggest strong action.)

2. Contrast the verbs in this paper with some from a book by Janell Cannon or one by William Steig. List a few favorite verbs your students hear. Then, compare the two lists. Do strong verbs make the writing more interesting? (Absolutely!)

3. Ask each student to choose one favorite new verb to use in his/her next piece of writing.

Advanced Extension

Sometimes, just replacing two or three words in a piece of writing can make the difference between mediocre word choice and striking, powerful word choice. Brainstorm alternatives for these words: *huge, carry, liked, big, good*. Then, replace the author's originals with your new words. Read your class revision aloud. How does it sound? Did a few words make a difference?

* See Teacher's Guide page 212 for a 6-point rubric. See page 206 for a 5-point rubric.

Sample Paper 13: Word Choice

A Birthday Gift

For my birthday, my sister gave me a huge jar of jellybeans. It weighed a lot! I could barely carry it to my room. I liked the bright colors of the jellybeans inside the big jar. When I opened the jar, I liked the smell. They smelled so, so good! I had to try one. It felt round and smooth. I put it in my mouth. Mmmmm. Yummy. So then, I wondered how another one would taste. I tried it. Mmmm. Good. Pretty soon, I had tried all the flavors! They were so good! I was stuffed, but I could not stop! I had the worst stomach ache I have had in my life. I gave the rest of the jellybeans back to my sister.

Think about the paper. Does the writer use new and interesting words? Do you hear any strong verbs? Put a check (√) in the blank that shows what you think about this paper. Then, write the reason for your rating.

_____ **Made it!**

_____ **Getting there**...

_____ **It's a start.**

_____

_____

_____

_____

_____

_____

Sample Paper 14: Leprechauns

Objective

Students will learn that even a few striking phrases and strong verbs make word choice powerful.

Materials

Student Rubric for Word Choice (Teacher's Guide page 59)

Sample Paper 14: Leprechauns (Teacher's Guide pages 167–168 and/or Overhead 14)

Presenting and Responding to the Paper

1. Distribute copies of the sample paper and the Student Rubric for Word Choice. Use the rubric to focus students' attention on the key features of the trait of Word Choice—using words that paint a vivid picture in the reader's mind, avoiding repetition, using strong verbs, and stretching for new words. Review any of these concepts that your students do not understand: **words that help you picture things, repetition, strong verbs, stretching**.

2. Share the paper, reading aloud as students follow along. Don't hesitate to read the paper more than once during the lesson.

3. Ask students to look at their rubrics, mark their responses (individually) by putting a check in the appropriate blank, and write why they chose a particular rating.

4. Ask students to compare their responses with those of a partner. They should take a few minutes to talk about the paper and ask each other questions. Expect this process to be slow at first; they will talk more as time goes on.

5. After one or two minutes, ask for responses from the whole class. If you like, jot down some of their ideas on a separate overhead. It may be helpful to read the paper aloud a second time.

Discussing the Paper

Discuss the paper with the class. Ask students to say what ratings they gave the paper and why. The *why* is the most important part in deepening their understanding. Use the following questions to encourage class discussion:

- What are your favorite words in this paper? Let's read it again together and underline them as we go. (Do this, and then read the words back.)

- Do you see or hear any strong verbs? Let's name some. (Remind students, as necessary, what a verb is.)

- Is it easy to picture what the writer is talking about? What do you see in your mind when you listen to this paper?

Response to the Paper

This paper is at a strong level (**Made it!**). The writer uses many interesting words and phrases: *tiny green people, mom does not believe they exist, it's fun to pretend, very sneaky, silent as a cat creeping on her paws, shadows in the forest.* The piece has many strong verbs: *creep, seeking, follow, lead, spot, disappear.* The words make it easy to picture what the writer is telling us.

Extensions

1. Leprechauns are not real—so no one has ever actually seen one! But the writer does tell us they are tiny green people, they are sneaky, and they like to look for pots of gold. Is this enough information to let you draw a picture of a Leprechaun? Try it. Compare results. Talk about details you needed to make up for your pictures.

2. The writer uses the expression "silent as a cat creeping on her paws." Tell your students to act this out. How would it look if you were in the forest trying to be silent as a cat creeping on her paws?

Advanced Extension

Verbs may come more easily when a writer works on an "action" piece—a story about sports or adventure. Ask students to think of a situation involving movement: playing ball, swimming, walking, shopping, taking a ride, etc. Ask them to write a short paragraph (about 5 lines or more) about this experience, using as many verbs as possible. When they finish, share paragraphs and listen for strong verbs.

* See Teacher's Guide page 212 for a 6-point rubric. See page 206 for a 5-point rubric.

Sample Paper 14: Word Choice

Leprechauns

Have you ever heard of Leprechauns? There are tales about tiny green people who live in the woods in Ireland. Some people think they are real, but a lot of people do not. My mom does not believe they exist, but it's fun to pretend. Leprechauns are very tiny and very sneaky. They do not make noise, so they can creep up on you when you do not suspect them. They are always seeking pots of gold! Some people believe if you follow the Leprechauns, they will lead you to the gold at the end of the rainbow. You have to be silent as a cat creeping on her paws, or they will hear you. If they spot you, they suddenly disappear. So we can't be sure if Leprechauns are real. They might just be shadows in the forest.

Think about the paper. Does the writer use new and interesting words? Do you hear any strong verbs? Put a check (√) in the blank that shows what you think about this paper. Then, write the reason for your rating.

___ **Made it!**

___ **Getting there**...

___ **It's a start.**

_____

_____

_____

_____

_____

Sample Paper 15: My Room

Objective

Students will learn that some words (such as *big*, *nice*, and *stuff*) do not tell us very much, so they do not make for strong word choice.

Materials

Student Rubric for Word Choice (Teacher's Guide page 59)

Sample Paper 15: My Room (Teacher's Guide page 171 and/or Overhead 15)

Presenting and Responding to the Paper

1. Distribute copies of the sample paper and the Student Rubric for Word Choice. Use the rubric to focus students' attention on the key features of the trait of Word Choice—using words that paint a vivid picture in the reader's mind, avoiding repetition, using strong verbs, and stretching for new words. Review any of these concepts that your students do not understand: **words that help you picture things, repetition, strong verbs, stretching**.

2. Share the paper, reading aloud as students follow along. Don't hesitate to read the paper more than once during the lesson.

3. Ask students to look at their rubrics, mark their responses (individually) by putting a check in the appropriate blank, and write why they chose a particular rating.

4. Ask students to compare their responses with those of a partner. They should take a few minutes to talk about the paper and ask each other questions. Expect this process to be slow at first; they will talk more as time goes on.

5. After one or two minutes, ask for responses from the whole class. If you like, jot down some of their ideas on a separate overhead. It may be helpful to read the paper aloud a second time.

Discussing the Paper

Discuss the paper with the class. Ask students to say what ratings they gave the paper and why. The *why* is the most important part in deepening their understanding. Use the following questions to encourage class discussion:

- Do you hear any strong verbs? Let's list them. (*holds, sit, read*—these verbs are not very strong, but the piece has some verbs.)

- Does the writer use any words that you have heard a lot?

- When you hear words like *nice, neat,* and *stuff,* is it easy or hard to picture what the writer is talking about? (This is a difficult question for young writers, and one you may need to return to.)

- Can you see the writer's room in your mind? What do you want to know?

Response to the Paper

This paper is at a beginning level (**It's a start**). The writer seems to like his/her room, but does not tell us anything specific: size, color, what is in the room (except a bed and TV), etc. Many words—*nice, like, big, stuff, neat*—are so vague that it is hard to picture the room or to tell exactly what it is like to be there. Use of these vague words weakens the writing.

Extensions

1. See if your students can identify three or more fuzzy words from "My Room." Read the piece aloud again if that helps.

2. Brainstorm some replacement words for the fuzzy words you identified. Replace one or two words in "My Room" with stronger choices. Then, read your class revision aloud. What difference do those new words make?

3. Ask students to look at a piece of writing that they have recently worked on. Is there one word that they could replace with a stronger word?

Advanced Extension

Ask students to choose one room within their home that they could write a short paragraph about. Before writing, encourage students to brainstorm five or more words that describe this room. Then, tell them to write. Students may draw a picture to accompany the paragraph. Afterwards, ask them to return to their writing to see if they want to add any details.

* See Teacher's Guide page 212 for a 6-point rubric. See page 206 for a 5-point rubric.

Sample Paper 15: Word Choice

My Room

My room is nice. I like it a lot. It is big but not too big. It holds all my stuff. My bed is nice and soft. If you sit on it, you will not want to get up for a long time! In my room you can read or play. You can do a lot of stuff. I think my room is neat. It is my favorite place.

Think about the paper. Does it have new and interesting words? Does it have strong verbs? Put a check (√) in the blank that shows what you think about this paper. Then, write the reason for your rating.

___ **Made it!**

___ **Getting there**...

___ **It's a start.**

_____

_____

_____

_____

Sample Paper 16: Gross, Gross, Gross!

Objective

Students will learn that specific words make word choice stronger.

Materials

Student Rubric for Word Choice (Teacher's Guide page 59)

Sample Paper 16: Gross, Gross, Gross! (Teacher's Guide pages 174–175 and/or Overhead 16)

Presenting and Responding to the Paper

1. Distribute copies of the sample paper and the Student Rubric for Word Choice. Use the rubric to focus students' attention on the key features of the trait of Word Choice—using words that paint a vivid picture in the reader's mind, avoiding repetition, using strong verbs, and stretching for new words. Review any of these concepts that your students do not understand: **words that help you picture things, repetition, strong verbs, stretching**.

2. Share the paper, reading aloud as students follow along. Don't hesitate to read the paper more than once during the lesson.

3. Ask students to look at their rubrics, mark their responses (individually) by putting a check in the appropriate blank, and write why they chose a particular rating.

4. Ask students to compare their responses with those of a partner. They should take a few minutes to talk about the paper and ask each other questions. Expect this process to be slow at first; they will talk more as time goes on.

5. After one or two minutes, ask for responses from the whole class. If you like, jot down some of their ideas on a separate overhead. It may be helpful to read the paper aloud a second time.

Discussing the Paper

Discuss the paper with the class. Ask students to say what ratings they gave the paper and why. The *why* is the most important part in deepening their understanding. Use the following questions to encourage class discussion:

• What, specifically, does the writer say to make you think mold is gross?

• Do you have a favorite word in this piece? Let's read it again, and list some.

• When the writer talks about "day-old greasy liver," can you picture it? Do you almost feel like you can smell and taste it? Is this good word choice?

• The writer says mold in the shower can "ooze between your toes." What does oozing look and feel like? Is this a good verb?

Response to the Paper

This paper is at a strong level (**Made it!**). The writer uses many strong, specific words and phrases to get the main idea across: *day-old greasy liver, socks hiding in your closet, green, slimy, stinky mold, bunches of dirty socks, ooze between your toes, mold is quiet, stay dry and keep moving*. The language is colorful and playful; it makes the reading fun.

Extensions

1. Some people object to the word *gross*. They think it is used so much it has lost its meaning. Another word for *gross* is *foul*. What if this paper were called "Foul, Foul, Foul!" Try reading it aloud, substituting the word *foul* for *gross*. Then, take a vote. How many like *foul* better?

2. *Ooze* is a colorful verb. Ask students to try drawing a picture of mold *oozing* between toes. Do the pictures capture the meaning?

3. Here are some other words that mean almost the same thing as *ooze*: *flow, seep, trickle, drizzle, dribble, drip*. Share this list with students, and make a "Means the Same" poster for borrowing. Do the same thing with other words.

Advanced Extension

Sometimes it's fun to write about things that are "gross," such as garbage! If you have access to a copy, share Shel Silverstein's playful poem "Sarah Cynthia Sylvia Stout Would not Take the Garbage Out." Notice the sensory details. After reading, talk about these sensory details, and ask students to write a sensory poem about something gross—or wonderful!

* See Teacher's Guide page 212 for a 6-point rubric. See page 206 for a 5-point rubric.

Sample Paper 16: Word Choice

Gross, Gross, Gross!

What is the grossest thing in the whole world? Is it day-old greasy liver? Is it dirty socks hiding in your closet? No! It's mold. Green, slimy, stinky mold is grosser than bunches of dirty socks or even liver. Mold grows any place it is damp. Mold will grow inside your washing machine! You can't see it because it's dark in there. But you can smell it. Yuck. It even grows on the floor of your shower where it could ooze between your toes. Mold is quiet so you never see it coming. It can make moms scream. Aaaaaaaah!! There is one good thing about mold. It is very, very slow. My advice is to stay dry and keep moving. Then, the mold can't catch you!

Think about the paper. Does the writer use new or interesting words? Does the writer use any strong verbs? Put a check (√) in the blank that shows what you think about this paper. Then, write the reason for your rating.

_____ **Made it!**

_____ **Getting there**...

_____ **It's a start.**

_____

_____

_____

_____

_____

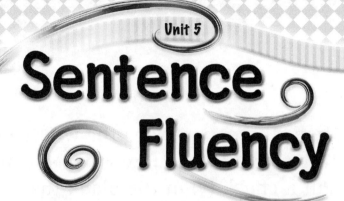

Sentence Fluency

Sample Paper 17: Elephants

Students will learn that sentence variety adds to fluency.

Student Rubric for Sentence Fluency (Teacher's Guide page 77)

Sample Paper 17: Elephants (Teacher's Guide pages 178–179 and/or Overhead 17)

Presenting and Responding to the Paper

1. Distribute copies of the sample paper and the Student Rubric for Sentence Fluency. Use the rubric to focus students' attention on the key features of the trait of Sentence Fluency—variety in sentence length and sentence beginnings, a smooth flow, and enough text (about four sentences or more) to give the reader a feeling for the flow. Review any of these concepts that your students do not understand: **different lengths, different beginnings, easy to read aloud, length**.

2. Share the paper, reading aloud as students follow along. Don't hesitate to read the paper more than once during the lesson.

3. Ask students to look at their rubrics, mark their responses (individually) by putting a check in the appropriate blank, and write why they chose a particular rating.

4. Ask students to compare their responses with those of a partner. They should take a few minutes to talk about the paper and ask each other questions. Expect this process to be slow at first; they will talk more as time goes on.

5. After one or two minutes, ask for responses from the whole class. If you like, jot down some of their ideas on a separate overhead. It may be helpful to read the paper aloud a second time.

© Great Source. Copying is prohibited.

176 Unit 5: Sample Papers

Discussing the Paper

Discuss the paper with the class. Ask students to say what ratings they gave the paper and why. The *why* is the most important part in deepening their understanding. Use the following questions to encourage class discussion:

- When you listened to the paper, did it sound smooth or bumpy?

- Did you hear many different sentence beginnings? Let's read it again and notice the first two words in each sentence. Underline those as we go along.

- There is one short sentence in this paper. It only has four words. Can you find it? One sentence in this paper has 16 words. Can anyone find it? If not, let them guess which one it is.

On the radio, you hear some fast songs and some slow songs. Is the variety good? What if every sentence in a book were exactly the same length?

Response to the Paper

This paper is at a strong level (**Made it!**). Sentences are highly varied, both in length and in the way they begin. This adds interest to the text and makes it easier to listen to. In addition, the paper is easy to read aloud. It flows right along, with no bumpy spots. It is well over four sentences long, so it is easy to get a feeling for the fluency—like a long song on the radio.

Extensions

1. Pick out one sentence with an unusual beginning: e.g., *Of all the animals in the world, my favorite is the elephant.* Ask students to write one sentence (on any topic) imitating this one. If you like, use this imitative sentence as the beginning of a longer writing piece.

2. Ask students to look at any piece of their writing and to underline the first two words. How much variety do they see? If many sentences are alike, ask students to change just one or two sentence beginnings to add variety. Then, read this revision aloud. How does it sound now?

Advanced Extension

Oral reading is critical to building fluency skills. Ask for volunteers to read "Elephants" aloud. Invite them to use a lot of expression! Divide the piece into two, three, or four parts for oral reading—but no more. It is important for students to read more than one sentence to build fluency skills.

* See Teacher's Guide page 213 for a 6-point rubric. See page 207 for a 5-point rubric.

Sample Paper 17: SENTENCE FLUENCY

Elephants

Of all the animals in the world, my favorite is the elephant. I like elephants for many reasons. For one thing, they are very smart. Elephants in Africa can tell when rain is coming. They smell the rain with their trunks. They also know when danger is near. If a lion is close, they will warn each other. Lions sometimes attack baby elephants. Another thing I like about elephants is how they care for each other. Mother elephants wash their babies and play with them. They stroke them with their trunks. If the mother elephant dies, other elephants in the herd will take care of the baby. Elephants are funny, too. They have water fights, just like kids. If you think about it, elephants are a lot like people.

name: .... date: ....

Think about the paper. Does it sound smooth or bumpy? Do many sentences begin in different ways? Put a check (√) in the blank that shows what you think about this paper. Then, write the reason for your rating.

___ **Made it!**

___ **Getting there**...

___ **It's a start.**

_____

_____

_____

_____

_____

_____

Sample Paper 18: Tiny

Students will learn that moderate variety in sentence length and variety in sentence beginnings make for strong fluency.

Materials

Student Rubric for Sentence Fluency (Teacher's Guide page 77)

Sample Paper 18: Tiny (Teacher's Guide page 182 and/or Overhead 18)

Presenting and Responding to the Paper

1. Distribute copies of the sample paper and the Student Rubric for Sentence Fluency. Use the rubric to focus students' attention on the key features of the trait of Sentence Fluency—variety in sentence length and sentence beginnings, a smooth flow, and enough text (about four sentences or more) to give the reader a feeling for the flow. Review any of these concepts that your students do not understand: **different lengths, different beginnings, easy to read aloud, length**.

2. Share the paper, reading aloud as students follow along. Don't hesitate to read the paper more than once during the lesson.

3. Ask students to look at their rubrics, mark their responses (individually) by putting a check in the appropriate blank, and write they chose a particular rating.

4. Ask students to compare their responses with those of a partner. They should take a few minutes to talk about the paper and ask each other questions. Expect this process to be slow at first; they will talk more as time goes on.

5. After one or two minutes, ask for responses from the whole class. If you like, jot down some of their ideas on a separate overhead. It may be helpful to read the paper aloud a second time.

Discussing the Paper

Discuss the paper with the class. Ask students to say what ratings they gave the paper and why. The *why* is the most important part in deepening their understanding. Use the following questions to encourage class discussion:

• Does the paper "Tiny" sound smooth or bumpy?

• Does the writer begin sentences in different ways? Let's look and listen one more time. Underline the first two words as you go. What do you notice?

• What is the shortest sentence you can find? How many words does it have?

• Who can find a long sentence? How many words does it have?

Response to the Paper

This paper is at a strong level (**Made it!**). Although this paper does not have quite as much variety as "Elephants" (Sample Paper 17), it is still highly varied, both in sentence lengths and in sentence beginnings. It is smooth and easy to read aloud or to listen to.

Extensions

1. Choose one sentence from the paper to use as a model. Ask students to write a similar sentence. Use this as the beginning of a longer piece (3–4 sentences or more). Ask students to try to make every sentence begin differently.

2. Now, try the same activity with a picture book. Extend the first sentence (the modeled sentence) into three or four, trying for variety in beginnings.

Advanced Extension

Reading with inflection requires identifying the most important words in a sentence. Try this with the sentences in "Tiny." For each sentence, pick one or two words that are important which could get special emphasis when you read. Underline them. Then, ask students to try reading the sentences aloud, emphasizing the underlined words. See if you hear the fluency coming out. Here are some key words marked for you as an example:

Our cat's name is **Tiny** because she is so **small**. Even though she is **small**, she had **kittens** last week. It was a total **surprise**! They were so **little**! Of course, I knew they would be **small**, but they were so small you could hold two in one **hand**.

* See Teacher's Guide page 213 for a 6-point rubric. See page 207 for a 5-point rubric.

Sample Paper 18: SENTENCE FLUENCY

Tiny

Our cat's name is Tiny because she is so small. Even though she is small, she had kittens last week. It was a total surprise! They were so little! Of course, I knew they would be small, but they were so small you could hold two in one hand. At first, they did not have fur. They just had smooth pink skin with some fuzz like a peach. They mewed so softly you had to put your ear real close to hear it. Tiny was proud of her three kittens. She pranced all over the place! When they nursed, she would purr like a little engine.

Think about the paper. Does it sound smooth or bumpy? Put a check (√) in the blank that shows what you think about this paper.

___ **Made it!**

___ **Getting there**...

___ **It's a start.**

Sample Paper 19: Fun Land

Objective

Students will learn that when most sentences are the same length and begin the same way, the piece is not fluent.

Materials

Student Rubric for Sentence Fluency (Teacher's Guide page 77)

Sample Paper 19: Fun Land (Teacher's Guide page 185 and/or Overhead 19)

Presenting and Responding to the Paper

1. Distribute copies of the sample paper and the Student Rubric for Sentence Fluency. Use the rubric to focus students' attention on the key features of the trait of Sentence Fluency—variety in sentence length and sentence beginnings, a smooth flow, and enough text (about four sentences or more) to give the reader a feeling for the flow. Review any of these concepts that your students do not understand: **different lengths, different beginnings, easy to read aloud, length**.

2. Share the paper, reading aloud as students follow along. Don't hesitate to read the paper more than once during the lesson.

3. Ask students to look at their rubrics, mark their responses (individually) by putting a check in the appropriate blank, and write why they chose a particular rating.

4. Ask students to compare their responses with those of a partner. They should take a few minutes to talk about the paper and ask each other questions. Expect this process to be slow at first; they will talk more as time goes on.

5. After one or two minutes, ask for responses from the whole class. If you like, jot down some of their ideas on a separate overhead. It may be helpful to read the paper aloud a second time.

Discussing the Paper

Discuss the paper with the class. Ask students to say what ratings they gave the paper and why. The *why* is the most important part in deepening their understanding. Use the following questions to encourage class discussion:

• Does this paper sound smooth or bumpy when you listen to it?

• Do many sentences start the same way? Let's look again. Underline the first two words as I read it with you. Now, what do you think?

• Try reading this paper aloud to your partner. Read as much as you can in one minute. What do you notice? (Students may notice similarities in sentence beginnings or in length or the general choppiness of the piece.)

Response to the Paper

This paper is at a beginning level (**It's a start**). The writer has put something on paper and does write in sentences. This is good. The sentences are almost all the same length and begin the same way, but just a few small changes could make this piece fluent.

Extensions

1. Pull out every sentence that begins with "We." Give each one to a pair of students. See if they can reword the sentence so it begins in another way. (This is a challenging task, so do not be concerned if they cannot do it the first time.) Provide help, if needed. Try to come up with at least three sentences that begin differently. Then, read your revision aloud.

2. Combining two choppy sentences is almost always a cure for low fluency. Try combining these two, with your students' help: *We were so tired that night! We went right to sleep!* Read your combined revision aloud to hear the increased smoothness! (Repeat this lesson often, using other examples. It gives students an important tool for building fluency.)

Advanced Extension

When students are ready, have them work in pairs to revise this piece for fluency. Give them some hints. Change two or more sentence beginnings. Try to combine some sentences, changing two short, choppy sentences into one longer, flowing sentence. Then, ask them to read their revisions aloud, as other students listen to the difference.

* See Teacher's Guide page 213 for a 6-point rubric. See page 207 for a 5-point rubric.

Sample Paper 19: SENTENCE FLUENCY

Fun Land

We went to Fun Land for our vacation. We left in July. We came home in July. We stayed for four nights. We stayed in our cousin's house. Our cousin's house is in Florida. We went on a giant roller coaster. It was very scary. We went upside down. We were so tired that night! We went right to sleep!

Think about the paper. Does it sound smooth or bumpy? Do sentences begin in different ways? Put a check (√) in the blank that shows what you think about this paper. Then, write the reason for your rating.

___ **Made it!**

___ **Getting there**...

___ **It's a start.**

_____

_____

_____

Sample Paper 20: My Cat Cleo

Objective

Students will learn that even a little variety can make the fluency stronger.

Materials

Student Rubric for Sentence Fluency (Teacher's Guide page 77)

Sample Paper 20: My Cat Cleo (Teacher's Guide page 188 and/or Overhead 20)

Presenting and Responding to the Paper

1. Distribute copies of the sample paper and the Student Rubric for Sentence Fluency. Use the rubric to focus students' attention on the key features of the trait of Sentence Fluency—variety in sentence length and sentence beginnings, a smooth flow, and enough text (about four sentences or more) to give the reader a feeling for the flow. Review any of these concepts that your students do not understand: **different lengths, different beginnings, easy to read aloud, length**.

2. Share the paper, reading aloud as students follow along. Don't hesitate to read the paper more than once during the lesson.

3. Ask students to look at their rubrics, mark their responses (individually) by putting a check in the appropriate blank, and write why they chose a particular rating.

4. Ask students to compare their responses with those of a partner. They should take a few minutes to talk about the paper and ask each other questions. Expect this process to be slow at first; they will talk more as time goes on.

5. After one or two minutes, ask for responses from the whole class. If you like, jot down some of their ideas on a separate overhead. It may be helpful to read the paper aloud a second time.

Discussing the Paper

Discuss the paper with the class. Ask students to say what ratings they gave the paper and why. The *why* is the most important part in deepening their understanding. Use the following questions to encourage class discussion:

- How does "My Cat Cleo" sound when it is read aloud? Is it smooth or bumpy?
- Do many sentences begin the same way? Which words does the writer use most often to begin sentences?
- How long is the shortest sentence you can find?
- Are there any really long sentences? How could you make some longer sentences?

Response to the Paper

This paper is at a mid-point level (**Getting there**...). The first part of the paper is choppy with short sentences, many of which begin with "She." In the second part, though, the writer begins to stretch the sentences out and varies the beginnings. It is easy to hear this difference when reading aloud. The increased fluency in the second part moves the paper to the **Getting there**... level.

Extensions

1. Read "My Cat Cleo" aloud followed by "Tiny" (Sample Paper 18). Listen to the differences, and talk about them. If your students are ready, ask them to do some of the reading. Otherwise, you can do it.

2. It is possible to combine all of the first four sentences into one. See if your students can do this, working in pairs. Tell them they get one point for each sentence they combine. So, if they combine all four (into one), they get three points, all four into two, two points, and all four into three, one point.

Advanced Extension

Ask students, working in teams of two, to revise this paper for fluency by eliminating "She" as a sentence beginning. It is fine to use any other sentence beginning so long as *no more than three* sentences in the whole piece begin the same way. Remind students of the keys to revision in fluency: change sentence beginnings and combine sentences. You may also wish to suggest some other possible ways to start sentences: *When...If...I...My cat...It...Sometimes...Of course....*

* See Teacher's Guide page 213 for a 6-point rubric. See page 207 for a 5-point rubric.

© Great Source. Copying is prohibited.

Sample Paper 20: Sentence Fluency

My Cat Cleo

I have a cat. Her name is Cleo. She is black. She has small white feet. She also has a white ear. She loves tuna. She is always hungry. Cleo sleeps a lot. She likes to sleep on my bed, right by my head! Cleo likes her ears scratched. She hunts for mice, and sometimes she eats them. It is disgusting! She also hunts for spiders. She does not eat spiders, though. I love Cleo, because she is my friend.

Think about the paper. Does it sound smooth or bumpy? Do many sentences begin in different ways? Put a check (√) in the blank that shows what you think about this paper. Then, write the reason for your rating.

___ **Made it!**

___ **Getting there...**

___ **It's a start.**

_____

_____

Conventions

Sample Paper 21: The Long Trip

Objective

Students will learn that when a writer overlooks mistakes in the writing, the text is harder for a reader to get through.

Materials

Student Rubric for Conventions (Teacher's Guide page 95)

Sample Paper 21: The Long Trip (Teacher's Guide page 191 and/or Overhead 21)

Presenting and Responding to the Paper

1. Distribute copies of the sample paper and the Student Rubric for Conventions. Use the rubric to focus students' attention on the key features of the trait of Conventions—looking the paper over, putting spaces between words, and correctly using simple conventions of spelling, capitalization, and punctuation. Review any of these concepts that your students do not understand: **looking the paper over, spaces between words, correct conventions**.

2. Share the paper, reading aloud as students follow along. Don't hesitate to read the paper more than once during the lesson.

3. Ask students to look at their rubrics, mark their responses (individually) by putting a check in the appropriate blank, and write why they chose a particular rating.

4. Ask students to compare their responses with those of a partner. They should take a few minutes to talk about the paper and ask each other questions. Expect this process to be slow at first; they will talk more as time goes on.

5. After one or two minutes, ask for responses from the whole class. If you like, jot down some of their ideas on a separate overhead. It may be helpful to read the paper aloud a second time.

Discussing the Paper

Discuss the paper with the class. Ask students to say what ratings they gave the paper and why. The *why* is the most important part in deepening their understanding. Use the following questions to encourage class discussion:

• Did you notice any errors in this paper? Some? A lot?

• What kinds of errors did you spot? See how many you can point out.

• When a writer makes errors, does your reading rate slow down? Why?

Response to the Paper

This paper is at a mid-point level (**Getting there . . .**). The errors do not seriously get in the way, but there are many things to correct (11 errors). Following is a corrected version with errors marked in bold. Repeated words that need to be deleted and inserted word space appear in brackets.

I drove to **C**alifornia with my mom **[#]** and dad. It was a long trip. Do you lik**e** sitting in the back seat**?** I don't! **T**hat trip **[trip]** took forever. I was hungry or thirsty most **of** the time. Also, my legs got very cramped. I have decided **I** do not like long trips that much. Do you**?**

Extensions

1. Have students, working with partners, correct the errors in the first sentence only. Add more sentences to the task only if time permits.

2. Tell students to review a piece of their own writing to see if they can find and correct two or three errors. Students who cannot find two errors should check with you or with a partner.

3. Ask how many students remember to write on every other line to leave room for making corrections.

Advanced Extension

Ask students to correct as many errors as they can in the paper. See how many they can correct on their own, and then go through it together, correcting each mistake.

* See Teacher's Guide page 214 for a 6-point rubric. See page 208 for a 5-point rubric.

Sample Paper 21: CONVENTIONS

The Long Trip

I drove to california with my momand dad. It was a long trip? Do you lik sitting in the back seat. I don't! that trip trip took forever. I was hungry or thirsty most the time Also, my legs got very cramped. I have decided i do not like long trips that much. Do you

Think about the paper. Did you see or hear many mistakes? What kinds of mistakes? Put a check (√) in the blank that shows what you think about this paper. Then, write the reason for your rating.

___ **Made it!**

___ **Getting there . . .**

___ **It's a start.**

_____

_____

_____

_____

Sample Paper 22: Feeding the Chickens

Objective

Students will learn that taking time to check for and correct errors makes writing easier to read.

Materials

Student Rubric for Conventions (Teacher's Guide page 95)

Sample Paper 22: Feeding the Chickens (Teacher's Guide page 194 and/or Overhead 22)

Presenting and Responding to the Paper

1. Distribute copies of the sample paper and the Student Rubric for Conventions. Use the rubric to focus students' attention on the key features of the trait of Conventions—looking the paper over, writing left to right, putting spaces between words, and using simple conventions of spelling, capitalization, and punctuation correctly. Review any of these concepts that your students do not understand: **looking the paper over, spaces between words, correct conventions**.

2. Share the paper, reading aloud as students follow along. Don't hesitate to read the paper more than once during the lesson.

3. Ask students to look at their rubrics, mark their responses (individually) by putting a check in the appropriate blank, and write why they chose a particular rating.

4. Ask students to compare their responses with those of a partner. They should take a few minutes to talk about the paper and ask each other questions. Expect this process to be slow at first; they will talk more as time goes on.

5. After one or two minutes, ask for responses from the whole class. If you like, jot down some of their ideas on a separate overhead. It may be helpful to read the paper aloud a second time.

Discussing the Paper

Discuss the paper with the class. Ask students to say what ratings they gave the paper and why. The *why* is the most important part in deepening their understanding. Use the following questions to encourage class discussion:

• Did you notice any errors in this paper? Some? A lot?

• What kinds of errors did you spot? See how many you can point out.

• When a writer makes errors, can it slow down your reading? Why?

Response to the Paper

This paper is at a mid-point level (**Getting there . . .**). As with the previous sample, there are 11 errors. Although the errors do not affect the meaning, they are distracting enough to be noticeable. They show that the writer is still working on control of conventions or just looked quickly at the paper and missed some things. Following is a corrected version with corrections marked in bold. Deleted words (those that were repeated) appear in brackets [ ], as do inserted word spaces.

My grandma lives [**#**] on a farm. **S**he and my grandpa have [**#**] chickens. One day when [**when**] I visited them, I got to fe**e**d the chickens. **T**hey eat grain. Grandma gave me a basket with some grain in [**#**] it. **I** scooped up one handful of grain at a time. I tossed it on the ground and th**e** chickens came running! I was afraid they would peck my feet, but they didn't. They j**u**st wanted their grain.

Extensions

1. Some editors find it helpful to look for one kind of mistake at a time. Ask your students to do this. For some young editors, a step-by-step approach is helpful.

2. Ask students to review a piece of their own writing to see if they can find and correct two or three errors. Students who cannot find two errors should check with you or with a partner.

3. Remind students to read their own writing aloud to listen for errors.

Advanced Extension

Ask students to correct as many errors as they can in the paper. See how many they can correct on their own, and then go through it together, correcting each mistake. If you have already done this text as a class, give students a different piece.

* See Teacher's Guide page 214 for a 6-point rubric. See page 208 for a 5-point rubric.

Sample Paper 22: CONVENTIONS

Feeding the Chickens

My grandma liveson a farm. she and my grandpa havechickens. One day when when i visited them, I got to fed the chickens. they eat grain Grandma gave me a basket with some grain init. i scooped up one handful of grain at a time. I tossed it on the ground and th chickens came running! I was afraid they would peck my feet, but they didn't. They jist wanted their grain.

Think about the paper. Did you see or hear many mistakes? Put a check (√) in the blank that shows what you think about this paper. Then, write the reason for your rating.

___ **Made it!**

___ **Getting there . . .**

___ **It's a start.**

_____

_____

_____

Sample Paper 23: Sunburn

Objective

Students will learn that too many mistakes can *really* slow a reader down.

Materials

Student Rubric for Conventions (Teacher's Guide page 95)

Sample Paper 23: Sunburn (Teacher's Guide page 197 and/or Overhead 23)

Presenting and Responding to the Paper

1. Distribute copies of the sample paper and the Student Rubric for Conventions. Use the rubric to focus students' attention on the key features of the trait of Conventions—looking the paper over, putting spaces between words, and using simple conventions of spelling, capitalization, and punctuation correctly. Review any of these concepts that your students do not understand: **looking the paper over, spaces between words, correct conventions**.

2. Share the paper, reading aloud as students follow along. Don't hesitate to read the paper more than once during the lesson.

3. Ask students to look at their rubrics, mark their responses (individually) by putting a check in the appropriate blank, and write why they chose a particular rating.

4. Ask students to compare their responses with those of a partner. They should take a few minutes to talk about the paper and ask each other questions. Expect this process to be slow at first; they will talk more as time goes on.

5. After one or two minutes, ask for responses from the whole class. If you like, jot down some of their ideas on a separate overhead. It may be helpful to read the paper aloud a second time.

Discussing the Paper

Discuss the paper with the class. Ask students to say what ratings they gave the paper and why. The *why* is the most important part in deepening their understanding. Use the following questions to encourage class discussion:

• Did you notice more errors in this paper than you have seen in others?

• What kinds of errors did you spot? See how many you can point out.

• Does it help to use your ears and eyes when looking for errors? Why?

Response to the Paper

This paper is at a beginning level (**It's a start**). It has enough errors to actually slow a reader down (20 total). Following is a copy of the paper with corrections marked in bold. Eliminated words (those that were repeated in the original) and inserted word space are marked in brackets [ ]:

Did you ever g**e**t a sunburn**?** **L**ast summer, we **[we]** visited my grandpa in **F**lorida. We spent the whole day **on** the beach. **I** ran around and **[#]** had fun. I did **not** think about th**e** sun. **Wh**en **I** got home, my mom asked **how** I got so red**?** I went to **[to]** look in the mirror. My face was **[was]** lik**e** a cherry. **I** couldn't even believe it was me! **S**he asked if I had used sunscreen. I said, "What is it?" **E**veryone laughed.

Extensions

1. Ask students to circle every mistake they spot. Then, ask them to count how many they circled. Did anyone come close to the total of 20? If no one found at least six, ask students to look again, this time with a partner.

2. Tell one partner in each pair to read the paper aloud as the other person hunts for errors. They need to read slowly so the editor can concentrate!

3. Remind students to read silently and aloud when looking for errors.

Advanced Extension

Try editing teams. One team looks just for lower case "i." Other teams look just for missing capital letters or for spelling errors. When teams finish their work, they should report their findings to the class. See if other students spotted anything the teams missed!

* See Teacher's Guide page 214 for a 6-point rubric. See page 208 for a 5-point rubric.

name: .... date: ....

Sample Paper 23: CONVENTIONS

Sunburn

Did you ever git a sunburn. last summer, we we visited my grandpa in florida. We spent the whole day the beach. i ran around andhad fun. I did not think about th sun. wen i got home, my mom asked hou I got so red. I went to to look in the mirror My face was was lik a cherry. i couldn't even believe it was me! she asked if I had used sunscreen. I said, "What is it?" everyone laughed.

Think about the paper. Does it have a few errors, some errors, or many errors? Put a check (√) in the blank that shows what you think about this paper. Then, write the reason for your rating.

___ **Made it!**

___ **Getting there . . .**

___ **It's a start.**

_____

_____

Unit 6: Sample Papers **197**

Sample Paper 24: A Day to Remember

Objective

Students will learn that even a few errors can slow a reader down.

Materials

Student Rubric for Conventions (Teacher's Guide page 95)

Sample Paper 24: A Day to Remember (Teacher's Guide page 200 and/or Overhead 24)

Presenting and Responding to the Paper

1. Distribute copies of the sample paper and the Student Rubric for Conventions. Use the rubric to focus students' attention on the key features of the trait of Conventions—looking the paper over, putting spaces between words, and using simple conventions of spelling, capitalization, and punctuation correctly. Review any of these concepts that your students do not understand: **looking the paper over, spaces between words, correct conventions**.

2. Share the paper, reading aloud as students follow along. Don't hesitate to read the paper more than once during the lesson.

3. Ask students to look at their rubrics, mark their responses (individually) by putting a check in the appropriate blank, and write why they chose a particular rating.

4. Ask students to compare their responses with those of a partner. They should take a few minutes to talk about the paper and ask each other questions. Expect this process to be slow at first; they will talk more as time goes on.

5. After one or two minutes, ask for responses from the whole class. If you like, jot down some of their ideas on a separate overhead. It may be helpful to read the paper aloud a second time.

Discussing the Paper

Discuss the paper with the class. Ask students to say what ratings they gave the paper and why. The *why* is the most important part in deepening their understanding. Use the following questions to encourage class discussion:

• Did you notice more errors in this paper than you have seen in other papers?

• What kinds of errors did you spot? See how many you can point out.

• Does it help to use your ears and your eyes when you look for errors? Why?

Response to the Paper

This paper is at a developing level (**Getting there . . .**). It has *just enough* errors to make them noticeable (only 8 total), and many things are done correctly. Just a few corrections would boost this paper into the **Made it!** (strong) category. Following is a copy of the paper with corrections marked in bold. Eliminated words (those that were repeated in the original) are marked in brackets [ ]:

Once **I** got to fly in a balloon. This sounds like I'm making it up, but I'm not! It was **one** of those big balloons with a basket you **c**an sit in. We floated way up in the sky. We were so high we could see for a million miles. I could see farms. The animals wer**e** tiny, like toys. I could see little **c**ars on th**e** roads. The best thing was my house. It looked **[looked]** so small. I could not believe I lived in something so small. I felt like a bird flying through the sky**.**

Extensions

1. Ask students to circle every mistake they spot. Then, ask them to count how many they circled. Did anyone come close to the total of 8? If no one found at least 4, ask them to look again, this time with a partner.

2. Ask one partner in each pair to read the paper aloud as the other person hunts for errors. They need to read slowly so the editor can concentrate!

3. Ask students to make a personal editing list of two kinds of errors they catch most of the time and one thing they often miss. Remind them to look for that "one thing" as they review their own work.

Advanced Extension

Editing is like detective work. Ask volunteers to make Wanted Posters for some of the errors that give them trouble. The poster should say "Wanted for Text Vandalism" and should include the name of the error, a sample of the error, and how it looks corrected. Students might create faces to go with error names!

* See Teacher's Guide page 214 for a 6-point rubric. See page 208 for a 5-point rubric.

name: .... date: ....

Sample Paper 24: CONVENTIONS

A Day to Remember

Once i got to fly in a balloon. This sounds like I'm making it up, but I'm not! It was won of those big balloons with a basket you kan sit in. We floated way up in the sky. We were so high we could see for a million miles. I could see farms. The animals wer tiny, like toys. I could see little kars on th roads. The best thing was my house. It looked looked so small. I could not believe I lived in something so small. I felt like a bird flying through the sky?

Think about the paper. Did you see and hear many errors? Put a check (√) in the blank that shows what you think about this paper.

___ **Made it!**

___ **Getting there . . .**

___ **It's a start.**

Appendix:
Using 5-Point and 6-Point Rubrics

For your convenience, we have included in this appendix 5-point and 6-point teacher rubrics for each trait. Although we recommend using verbal descriptors with young writers, we have included in this appendix 5-point and 6-point teacher rubrics for each trait. The students can continue to use the student rubrics provided in the introduction to each unit in this Teacher's Guide, since the verbal descriptors are more developmentally appropriate for them. Of the two numbered rubrics, we prefer the 6-point scale; however, we recognize that many people use the 5-point scale.

All rubrics are essentially 3-point rubrics: weak, somewhat strong, and strong. On the 5-point rubric, these performance levels correspond to the scores of 1, 3, and 5 respectively. Only these three performance levels are fully defined. On the 6-point rubric, each level is divided into two parts, high and low. Thus, a score of 1 represents the lowest weak score, and a score of 2 is a somewhat higher weak score. Scores of 3 and 4 represent the two levels of the somewhat strong category; 5 and 6 are the two levels of strength. On the 6-point rubric, *all* performance levels are defined.

Our recommended primary level rubrics use descriptors. However, if you wish to use numbers (for grading purposes), the rubrics can easily be adapted to either 5-point or 6-point scales. As mentioned previously, we recommend the 6-point rubric. The "Made it!" level can be defined as a 5 or a 5–6 split, depending on the scale. The "Getting there…" level is a 3 on a 5-point scale, or a 3–4 split on a 6-point scale. The "It's a start." level is a 1 on a 5-point scale, or a 1–2 split on a 6-point scale. You do not need to worry about numbers unless you are using the scales for grading purposes and need a point total to compute grades.

Few differences exist conceptually between these rubrics. Remember that the key reason to use rubrics with students is to teach the concepts: *ideas, organization, voice, word choice, sentence fluency,* and *conventions.* We want students to understand what we mean, for example, by good *organization,* and one way of doing this is to have them score writing samples. The particular rubric used is less important than whether a student sees a paper as weak, strong, or somewhere between those two points. We want students to distinguish between writing that works and writing that needs revision; whether they define a strong performance as a 5 or 6 is much less important than their understanding of why a paper is strong or weak. The numbers are merely a kind of shorthand that allows students and teachers to discuss competency in simple terms.

We hope that these distinctions help clarify the very slight differences between these rubrics. Use the rubrics with which you are most familiar or with which you feel most comfortable. Regardless of your choice, you will be teaching your students about the basic components that define good writing—and that is what counts!

Ideas

5 Made it!

_____ The paper has a strong, easy-to-identify main message.

_____ The writer sticks with this main topic.

_____ The writer seems to know a lot about his/her topic.

_____ The writer consistently chooses interesting details.

_____ The paper is very clear; it is easy to understand.

4 Getting there PLUS

This paper has at least two elements of a 5 paper but could still use revision to expand or clarify the main message.

3 Getting there . . .

_____ The paper has an identifiable main message.

_____ The writer introduces one or more unrelated topics.

_____ The writer does not give enough information.

_____ The writer shares only one or two details about the main idea.

_____ In most cases, you can figure out what the writer is saying.

2 Start PLUS

The paper has a main message but no detail as yet. The writer needs more information or just needs to think more about the topic.

1 It's a start.

_____ The paper does not seem, as yet, to have a main message.

_____ The writer does not give enough information.

_____ The writer does not share details about the main idea.

_____ The writer's point, story, or main message is unclear.

Organization

5 Made it!

_____ The paper has a strong, logical sense of order. It is easy to follow.

_____ The writer sticks to the main idea; he/she does not meander.

_____ The beginning (lead) is compelling and draws the reader in.

_____ The ending fits the paper well and makes it feel finished.

4 Getting there PLUS

This paper has at least two elements of a 5 paper but could still use revision to tidy up the order or to strengthen the lead or conclusion.

3 Getting there . . .

_____ The paper has a reasonable sense of order; some details could be moved or eliminated altogether.

_____ Mostly, the writer sticks to the main idea but occasionally meanders.

_____ The paper has a beginning.

_____ The paper has an ending.

2 Start PLUS

The paper may have a recognizable beginning and/or ending, but what comes in between is either random or very hard to follow.

1 It's a start.

_____ Details seem random with no main idea.

_____ The writer meanders.

_____ The paper does not have any real beginning; it just starts.

_____ The paper does not have any real ending; it just stops.

Voice

5 Made it!
_____ This is a piece you will want to share aloud.

_____ The writing sounds like this individual writer.

_____ The writing is consistently lively and expressive.

_____ My paper shows feelings; the writer seems to care about the topic and to speak right to the audience.

4 Getting there PLUS
This paper has at least two elements of a 5 paper but could still use revision to strengthen the voice.

3 Getting there . . .
_____ There are moments you might share aloud.

_____ Here and there the writer's individual voice peeks through.

_____ There is at least a sentence, a word, or a phrase that stands out; it's lively and expressive—striking or different.

_____ At least one sentence shows engagement with the topic or sensitivity to the audience.

2 Start PLUS
The writing seems sincere and earnest, even if there are no read-aloud moments as of yet.

1 It's a start.
_____ This paper is not ready to be shared aloud—yet!

_____ It's hard to connect this writing with a particular writer.

_____ The writer has not put enough of him- or herself into the writing (yet) to make it lively and expressive.

_____ The paper does not reflect any engagement with the topic or audience—yet!

Word Choice

5 Made it!

_____ It is easy to picture what the writer is talking about.

_____ Repetition is rare. The writer finds that "just right" word.

_____ Strong verbs show action and give life to the piece.

_____ The writer stretches for new ways to express ideas.

_____ Sensory words add color and life throughout the piece.

4 Getting there PLUS

This paper has at least two elements of a 5 paper but could still use revision to strengthen the word choice.

3 Getting there . . .

_____ Most of the time, you can picture what the writer is saying.

_____ A few words are repeated; this does not impair meaning.

_____ Only one or two strong verbs show action.

_____ Once or twice the writer stretches for a fresh word.

_____ Sensory words or phrases are used at least once.

2 Start PLUS

The reader can make a good guess about the writer's message, despite fuzzy language, repetition, or lack of strong verbs.

1 It's a start.

_____ It is very difficult to picture what the writer is talking about.

_____ Many words are repeated.

_____ Strong verbs are not included in the piece as yet.

_____ The writer is not taking a risk with any new words yet.

_____ Sensory words might be helpful but are not used.

Sentence Fluency

5 Made it!

_____ This piece is very easy to read aloud; it has a natural flow.

_____ Many sentences begin in different ways.

_____ Long and short sentences blend, giving the text variety.

_____ The piece is long enough to allow fluency to build.

_____ The writer uses complete sentences.

4 Getting there <u>PLUS</u>

This paper has at least two elements of a 5 paper but could still use revision to strengthen the fluency.

3 Getting there . . .

_____ The piece is not difficult to read aloud.

_____ A few sentences begin in different ways.

_____ Some sentences are longer than others.

_____ The text is long enough to gain some fluency.

_____ The writer uses complete sentences in most cases.

2 Start <u>PLUS</u>

The reader can read the paper aloud with effort, but it is choppy with lack of whole sentences and repetition.

1 It's a start.

_____ The piece is difficult to read aloud.

_____ All sentences begin the same way and are about the same length.

OR

_____ The writer composed just one or two sentences.

_____ Sentences run together or are not complete.

Conventions

5 Made it! (Check 4 or more)

_____ Conventions come easily to this writer.

_____ The writer put spaces between words.

_____ The spelling is correct or easy to read.

_____ Punctuation is consistently used to end sentences.

_____ Capital letters are consistently used to start sentences.

4 Getting there PLUS

This paper has at least three elements of a 5 paper.

3 Getting there . . . (Check 4 or more)

_____ Conventions make the paper readable.

_____ The writer put spaces between most words.

_____ Most of the spelling is readable with attention.

_____ Punctuation is used to end most (or some) sentences.

_____ Capital letters are used to start most (or some) sentences.

2 Start PLUS

This paper has at least three elements of a 3 paper.

1 It's a start. (Check 3 or more)

_____ Conventions are very difficult for this writer.

_____ The writer often forgot to put spaces between words.

_____ A lot of the spelling is hard to read.

_____ Punctuation does not appear at the end of all sentences.

_____ Capital letters do not always begin sentences.

Ideas

6 Made it PLUS

This piece has all the elements of a 5 paper. In addition, the writer displays understanding of the topic and chooses "just right" details.

5 Made it!

_____ The paper has a strong, easy-to-identify main message.

_____ The writer sticks with this main topic.

_____ The writer seems to know a lot about his/her topic.

_____ The writer consistently chooses interesting details.

_____ The paper is very clear; it is easy to understand.

4 Getting there PLUS

This paper has at least two elements of a 5 paper but could still use revision to expand or clarify the main message.

3 Getting there . . .

_____ The paper has an identifiable main message.

_____ The writer may introduce one or more unrelated topics.

_____ The writer does not give enough information.

_____ The writer shares only one or two details about the main idea.

_____ In most cases, you can figure out what the writer is saying.

2 Start PLUS

The paper has a main message but no detail as yet. The writer needs more information or just needs to think more about the topic.

1 It's a start.

_____ The paper does not seem, as yet, to have a main message.

_____ The writer does not give enough information.

_____ The writer does not share details about the main idea.

_____ The writer's point, story, or main message is unclear.

Organization

6 Made it PLUS

This piece has all the elements of a 5 paper. In addition, the writer creates a striking lead and/or conclusion. The paper flows effortlessly from point to point.

5 Made it!

_____ The paper has a strong, logical sense of order. It is easy to follow.

_____ The writer sticks to the main idea; he/she does not meander.

_____ The beginning (lead) is compelling and draws the reader in.

_____ The ending fits the paper well and makes it feel finished.

4 Getting there PLUS

This paper has at least two elements of a 5 paper but could still use revision to tidy up the order or to strengthen the lead or conclusion.

3 Getting there . . .

_____ The paper has a reasonable sense of order; some details could be moved or eliminated altogether.

_____ Mostly, the writer sticks to the main idea, but occasionally meanders.

_____ The paper has a beginning.

_____ The paper has an ending.

2 Start PLUS

The paper may have a recognizable beginning and/or ending, but what comes in between is either random or very hard to follow.

1 It's a start.

_____ Details seem random with no main idea.

_____ The writer meanders.

_____ The paper does not have any real beginning; it just starts.

_____ The paper does not have any real ending; it just stops.

Voice

6 Made it <u>PLUS</u>

This piece has all the elements of a 5 paper. In addition, the writer creates a piece that demands to be read aloud. The piece abounds with honesty, enthusiasm, and individuality. It's unique.

5 Made it!

_____ This is a piece you will want to share aloud.

_____ The writing sounds like this individual writer.

_____ The writing is consistently lively and expressive.

_____ My paper shows feelings; the writer seems to care about the topic and to speak right to the audience.

4 Getting there <u>PLUS</u>

This paper has at least two elements of a 5 paper but could still use revision to strengthen the voice.

3 Getting there . . .

_____ There are moments you might share aloud.

_____ Here and there the writer's individual voice peeks through.

_____ There is at least a sentence, a word, or a phrase that stands out; it's lively and expressive—striking or different.

_____ At least one sentence shows engagement with the topic or sensitivity to the audience.

2 Start <u>PLUS</u>

The writing seems sincere and earnest, even if there are no read-aloud moments as of yet.

1 It's a start.

_____ This paper is not ready to be shared aloud—yet!

_____ It's hard to connect this writing with a particular writer.

_____ The writer has not put enough of him- or herself into the writing (yet) to make it lively and expressive.

_____ The paper does not reflect any engagement with the topic or audience—yet!

Word Choice

6 Made it <u>PLUS</u>

This piece has all the elements of a 5 paper. The word choice consistently creates strong images, boosts the voice, and enhances the writer's message.

5 Made it!

_____ It is easy to picture what the writer is talking about.

_____ Repetition is rare. The writer finds that "just right" word.

_____ Strong verbs show action and give life to the piece.

_____ The writer stretches for new ways to express ideas.

_____ Sensory words add color and life throughout the piece.

4 Getting there <u>PLUS</u>

This paper has at least two elements of a 5 paper but could still use revision to strengthen the word choice.

3 Getting there . . .

_____ Most of the time, you can picture what the writer is saying.

_____ A few words are repeated; this does not impair meaning.

_____ Only one or two strong verbs show action.

_____ Once or twice the writer stretches for a fresh word.

_____ Sensory words or phrases are used at least once.

2 Start <u>PLUS</u>

The reader can make a good guess about the writer's message, despite fuzzy language, repetition, or lack of strong verbs.

1 It's a start.

_____ It is very difficult to picture what the writer is talking about.

_____ Many words are repeated.

_____ Strong verbs are not included in the piece as yet.

_____ The writer is not taking a risk with any new words yet.

_____ Sensory words might be helpful but are not used.

Sentence Fluency

6 Made it PLUS

This piece has all the elements of a 5 paper. Plus, the length provides true fluency. The piece varies greatly in sentence length with almost every sentence beginning differently, clearly connecting ideas.

5 Made it!

_____ This piece is very easy to read aloud; it has a natural flow.

_____ Many sentences begin in different ways.

_____ Long and short sentences blend, giving the text variety.

_____ The piece is long enough to allow fluency to build.

_____ The writer uses complete sentences.

4 Getting there PLUS

This paper has at least two elements of a 5 paper but could still use revision to strengthen the fluency.

3 Getting there . . .

_____ The piece is not difficult to read aloud.

_____ A few sentences begin in different ways.

_____ Some sentences are longer than others.

_____ The text is long enough to gain some fluency.

_____ The writer uses complete sentences in most cases.

2 Start PLUS

The reader can read the paper aloud with effort, but it is choppy with lack of whole sentences and repetition.

1 It's a start.

_____ The piece is difficult to read aloud.

_____ All sentences begin the same way and are about the same length.

OR

_____ The writer composed just one or two sentences.

_____ Sentences run together or are not complete.

Conventions

6 Made it PLUS

This piece has all the elements of a 5 paper. Conventions are used with skill and control and help the reader to read the text aloud with expression, fluency, and voice. In addition, the writer may attempt use of some beyond-grade-level conventions: e.g., quotation marks, dashes, ellipses, semicolons.

5 Made it! (Check 4 or more)

_____ Conventions come easily to this writer.

_____ The writer put spaces between words.

_____ The spelling is correct or easy to read.

_____ Punctuation is consistently used to end sentences.

_____ Capital letters are consistently used to start sentences.

4 Getting there PLUS

This paper has at least three elements of a 5 paper.

3 Getting there . . . (Check 4 or more)

_____ Conventions make the paper readable.

_____ The writer put spaces between most words.

_____ Most of the spelling is readable with attention.

_____ Punctuation is used to end most (or some) sentences.

_____ Capital letters are used to start most (or some) sentences.

2 Start PLUS

It has at least three elements of a 3 paper.

1 It's a start. (Check 3 or more)

_____ Conventions are very difficult for this writer.

_____ The writer often forgot to put spaces between words.

_____ A lot of the spelling is hard to read.

_____ Punctuation does not appear at the end of all sentences.

_____ Capital letters do not always begin sentences.